BREATH
~as~
PRAYER

CALM YOUR ANXIETY, FOCUS YOUR MIND, AND RENEW YOUR SOUL

JENNIFER TUCKER

FOREWORD BY ANN VOSKAMP

THOMAS NELSON
Since 1798

PRESENTED TO

FROM

Breath As Prayer

© 2022 Jennifer Tucker

Published in Nashville, Tennessee, by Thomas Nelson. Thomas Nelson is a registered trademark of HarperCollins Christian Publishing, Inc.

Thomas Nelson titles may be purchased in bulk for educational, business, fundraising, or sales promotional use. For information, please e-mail SpecialMarkets@ThomasNelson.com.

The information in this book has been carefully researched by the authors and is intended to be a source of information only. Readers are urged to consult with their physicians or other professional advisors to address specific medical or other issues. The author and the publisher assume no responsibility for any injuries suffered or damages incurred during or as a result of the use or application of the information contained herein.

Unless otherwise noted, Scripture quotations taken from the Holy Bible, New Living Translation. © 1996, 2004, 2015 by Tyndale House Foundation. Used by permission of Tyndale House Publishers, Inc., Carol Stream, Illinois 60188. All rights reserved.

Scripture quotations marked NIV are taken from The Holy Bible, New International Version®, NIV®. Copyright © 1973, 1978, 1984, 2011 by Biblica, Inc.® Used by permission of Zondervan. All rights reserved worldwide. www. Zondervan.com. The "NIV" and "New International Version" are trademarks registered in the United States Patent and Trademark Office by Biblica, Inc.®

Scripture quotations marked CSB® are taken from the Christian Standard Bible®, Copyright © 2017 by Holman Bible Publishers. Used by permission. Christian Standard Bible® and CSB®, are federally registered trademarks of Holman Bible Publishers.

Scripture quotations marked ESV are taken from the ESV® Bible (The Holy Bible, English Standard Version®). Copyright © 2001 by Crossway, a publishing ministry of Good News Publishers. Used by permission. All rights reserved.

Scripture quotations marked THE MESSAGE are taken from THE MESSAGE. Copyright © 1993, 2002, 2018 by Eugene H. Peterson. Used by permission of NavPress. All rights reserved. Represented by Tyndale House Publishers, Inc.

Scripture quotations marked NASB are taken from the New American Standard Bible® (NASB). Copyright © 1960, 1962, 1963, 1968, 1971, 1972, 1973, 1975, 1977, 1995 by The Lockman Foundation. Used by permission. www. lockman.org

Any internet addresses, phone numbers, or company or product information printed in this book are offered as a resource and are not intended in any way to be or to imply an endorsement by Thomas Nelson, nor does Thomas Nelson vouch for the existence, content, or services of these sites, phone numbers, companies, or products beyond the life of this book.

ISBN 978-1-4002-3458-5 (hardcover)

ISBN 978-1-4002-3460-8 (audiobook)

ISBN 978-1-4002-3459-2 (eBook)

Printed in the United States of America

24 25 26 27 28 29 30   VER   25 24 23 22 21 20 19 18 17 16 15 14 13 12

To

Emma and Lilly

Being your mom is the
greatest joy of my life.

CONTENTS

FOREWORD

You can breathe relief.

You can know: The moment you fold your hands in prayer, a greater revolution begins than if you took up arms—and it begins in your heart.

The revolution begins right there, with your next heartbeat:

Your cries directly usher you immediately into the very presence of God. "I called to God, to my God I cried out . . . he heard me call; my cry brought me right into his presence—a private audience!" (2 Samuel 22:7 THE MESSAGE). Your prayers are more than a desperate thing; they are a transporting thing, the most important thing. Your prayers immediately relocate you to face the tender face of God. Your every breath—inhale, exhale—makes the sound of His name, is calling for Him—YHWH, YHWH.

And He who makes us

will make it

so we make it.

Make it to the next breath, to the next moment, to the next sunrise, to the next season, to the next step that will take us closer to home and Him.

When life leaves us gasping for air, prayer is how you grasp the steadying, sure hand of God.

You are going to make it—you are going to breathe through a story you desperately wanted to be different. To learn to breathe prayers through all the labor pains of living is to be delivered into peace.

Because the real purpose of prayer is not about convincing God to do what we want but about awakening to what God already is doing and doing that redemptive work with Him. Prayer is the subversive work that defies the lie that all that is happening is just what we see but trusts that underneath, and through everything, God's revolutionary and redeeming work is still victoriously happening.

"Anything is a blessing which makes us pray," writes Charles Spurgeon.

And as two friends who can testify to this truth, two mothers, two daughters of the King of kings, Jenn Tucker and I have long walked together through some achingly dark nights of the soul, standing with each other, kneeling with each other, grieving with each other, breathing prayers with each other, for each other, and the hard things become holy things as we bring them to Him.

Jenn is a genuine woman of the Word, a woman who trusts that God is trustworthy, that He communicates, and a life of intimately communicating with Him, and daily listening to Him, leads to a life of deeply fulfilling communion, even, especially, in crisis. This profoundly personal prayer journey Jenn invites all the weary on is one bore out of her own deep valleys, and she is an uncommonly kind guide and wise companion, breathing prayers with you every step of the long way through.

In the midst of your wounding trials and winding trails, she will gently take your hand, show you how to take the next deep breath, look up in the dark, and pray like Columba of Iona:

"Be a bright flame before me, O God
a guiding star above me.
Be a smooth path below me,
a kindly shepherd behind me
today, tonight, and forever.
Alone with none but you, my God,
I journey on my way;
what need I fear when you are near,
O Lord of night and day?
More secure am I within your hand
than if a multitude did round me stand.
Amen."

Whatever surrounds, God surrounds, closer than your next breath, your next heartbeat.

Short prayers, breath prayers, long soften your heart to surrender into the shape of God's hands. And when your heart is softly surrendered to God's, the revolution of all things wins freedom, wins real release from all fear. Love Himself is here.

Breathe.

Pray.

Breathe.

Pray.

When you live in prayer, you live in peace.

Your next breath can be your getaway to God, where you retreat into Him and the deepest peace you've even known.

Ann Voskamp

WHAT IS

Breath Prayer?

It was nearly 2 AM when they wheeled my daughter from the emergency room to her inpatient room on the fourth floor of a children's hospital in Atlanta. Outside the small window, city lights poked holes against the black veil of night and cast shadows on the wall above the bed. A too-big hospital gown fell loosely over her tired body, and wires strung from her chest to the monitors beside her bed, blinking with the rhythm of her heart as I held her hand and she drifted off to sleep. A hard vinyl couch beside the wall would be my bed as a nurse sat with us, checking in every fifteen minutes. My precious girl looked so small and frail in that hospital bed. She was sicker than we'd realized, and this latest crisis had left me overwhelmed and unsteady.

As I lay there in the darkness of that hospital room, my eyes welled with an overflow of pain and helplessness. The familiar signs of anxiety began to flood through my body. My chest grew tight and heavy, and my hands began to tremble as I struggled to catch my breath.

I felt small and scared and so very alone.

I tried to pray, but my mind was only filled with worry and fear. I lost my words.

I had nothing left to say, nothing left to pray.

As I grasped for hope and gasped for breath, I remembered: *There are words I can pray when I have no words to pray, when all I have to offer is my trembling breath.*

A few months earlier, I had read about breath prayers for the first time and was captivated. I wrote a few down and tucked them in my heart. And now, months later, the words of one of those prayers suddenly came to my mind. It was just a handful of words from Psalm 23, broken into two small lines. I took a deep breath, and as I inhaled, I tried to focus my mind on the words, "The Lord is my shepherd," and as I exhaled, I whispered, "I have all that I need." And again, breathing in deeply, I focused my thoughts on "The Lord is my shepherd," and then breathed out "I have all that I need."

As I focused on my breathing and the words of Scripture, my body calmed and my soul was reminded of a truth that will never change, no matter my circumstances: "The Lord is my shepherd"—even here in this hospital, next to my daughter hooked up to monitors. And "I have all that I need"—because even here, in the dark, I have Him. The good shepherd. The one who tenderly guides us and holds us when we're wounded and weary, the One who keeps watch over us through the night. He is all that I need.

That simple prayer helped quiet my worries and fears.

The deep breathing helped to calm the physical symptoms of my anxiety, and the prayer helped me to recenter my thoughts on Christ and His love for me, and I drifted off to sleep with a renewed peace.

In the weeks that followed, as I sat by my daughter's side day and night in that little room, I kept repeating short passages of Scripture to myself as I intentionally slowed my breathing, inhaling and exhaling to the rhythm of the Word. Breath prayers filled my days. Sometimes I'd walk the halls of the hospital, when I was feeling overwhelmed and anxiety was tugging hard at my heart, and I'd breathe slowly as I walked, repeating the words of a short prayer over and over like a steady rhythm of grace until my body calmed and peace once again returned.

The science of breathing and the practice of praying God's Word can work hand-in-hand to help calm your body and reorient your mind toward Christ.

Breath prayers changed me during those weeks. And they've continued to be a lifeline as I've walked through dark and difficult days since.

They've become a comfort to me, not just in times of high anxiety but on any day, strengthening both my body and soul by helping me tuck important truths in my heart and paving paths of peace in my mind.

I wrote this book because it's the book I needed when the walls of that hospital room were closing in and I struggled to breathe and didn't know what to pray. It's the book I need today, as worries and anxieties continue to press in and the days ahead remain uncertain. So I humbly offer these words from my own anxiety-prone soul to yours, as a friendly and compassionate guide to the simple but powerful technique of breath prayers. No matter what condition your mind and body are in right now, no matter the reason you've opened this book, I hope you will find grace in these pages and that breath prayer will open a door to an even deeper connection with the God who made you and loves you, the One who rescues you and redeems you, the One who is with you always, no matter what you are feeling.

UNDERSTANDING BREATH PRAYERS

Breath prayers combine two powerful tools that can help calm anxiety: the science of deep breathing and prayers of meditation on God's Word.

We often tend to separate science and faith as if they are contradictory forces at war with one another. But in reality, the science of the brain and body doesn't contradict the Word of God at all. If anything, it only further validates it.[1] It is God who created and designed our bodies after all.

Depending on your background, the concept of breathwork and meditation may initially give you pause. Perhaps it conjures images of a mystic meditating on a mountainside, or maybe it sounds like a new-age practice. Though many religions and spiritual practices use forms of meditation and breathing, breath prayers are different.

Breath prayers combine deep breathing exercises with prayers of meditation on God's Word to help calm your body while focusing your mind on truth.

Breath prayers aren't a cure for anxiety, nor are they a replacement for professional medical treatment or therapy. But they can be a powerful tool to add to your mental health toolkit. We all experience anxiety in some form throughout our lives. When prayed regularly, these prayers can transform how you respond to that anxiety and can help you experience a deep and abiding peace as you navigate the often-choppy waters of fear and worry.

Breath prayers

ARE:

- Short, mostly one-sentence prayers
- Rooted in Scripture
- Aligned with the rhythm of the breath: first half is prayed while inhaling, second half is prayed while exhaling
- Repeated several times for the purpose of meditating on God's Word by actively processing the words and reflecting on them
- Mind-FULL: focusing the mind on Christ and filling the mind with His Word
- Directed upward, to God

ARE NOT:

- A new-age, humanistic, self-healing practice
- Rooted in eastern spirituality or pagan practices
- A cure for all anxiety
- "Mantra Meditation" with the purpose of blotting out thoughts and repeating a word or phrase over and over until even that phrase loses all meaning
- Mindless: focused on emptying the mind to obtain inner peace
- Directed inward, to self

ANXIETY AND THE BODY

Worry and anxiety are common human experiences. Worry finds its home in our mind and is typically fueled by our thoughts and concerns about specific events or circumstances in our lives. We all worry, though some of us are admittedly bigger worriers than others. We may worry about our kids, our health, our relationships, our jobs, or even the future and things that haven't even happened yet. Life is full of stressful situations that can fill our minds with worry; and for many of us, that worry can quickly lead to its more intense counterpart, anxiety. Worry and anxiety are interrelated,[2] but where worry resides mainly in our minds, anxiety is worry we wear in our bodies. Anxiety manifests itself in physical symptoms that can be very uncomfortable.

The way our bodies process emotions and stressful situations is not an accident. God designed our bodies in intricately connected ways, and understanding how the body experiences anxiety is the first step to understanding how to calm it.

The autonomic nervous system, which includes the sympathetic and parasympathetic nervous systems, connects the brain to every internal organ and automatically regulates numerous body functions, including our response to stress and anxiety.[3]

When the body senses danger, the sympathetic nervous system is triggered to go into action. It acts like an accelerator, revving up our internal systems to respond.[4] Heart rate increases, breathing becomes more rapid, and the fight or flight response is activated. A whole series of complex responses happens almost instantaneously[5] while the "emotional brain" (the amygdala) takes over and bypasses the "thinking brain" (the prefrontal cortex),[6] making it very difficult to process thoughts rationally and maintain perspective. Have you ever noticed that it's difficult to think

Please note: There is a difference between anxiety (which we all experience) and anxiety disorders (which affect about 20 percent of the population).[7]

Anxiety is a temporary feeling of uneasiness or worry that has a specific source and the severity of the symptoms is typically in proportion to that cause. We all experience anxiety from time to time that is fueled by worry, stress, or fear over things that are both within and outside our control. This is a normal human experience.

Anxiety disorders are different. A person with an anxiety disorder experiences chronic anxiety that is often intense and disproportionate to the situation. They may even experience anxiety without any specific cause. There are many different kinds of anxiety disorders, each with different sets of physical and cognitive symptoms. If left untreated, anxiety disorders can grow more severe over time and can seriously impact a person's daily life.

When anxiety is mentioned in this book, it is referring to common, everyday anxiety. This book is not intended as a guide to treat or diagnose any medical or psychological conditions. If you are struggling with severe anxiety or experiencing other mental health symptoms that are interfering with your everyday life, please seek help from a trained and qualified professional. There is no shame in receiving care for your mental health. Mental health conditions are not a sign of weakness or a lack of faith. The brain is a complex organ prone to illness and disorder just like every other part of our fallen bodies.

And if you are experiencing thoughts of hopelessness or suicide, please call for immediate help: National Suicide Hotline, 1-800-273-8255

It's okay not to be okay. But there is help. You don't have to suffer alone.

when you're feeling an intense emotion like fear? You respond on pure instinct in those moments. Your "gut" reaction typically takes over, and you may even feel a bit out of control. This is by design, and it's a really good thing when faced with a dangerous threat.

Once the perceived danger has passed, the parasympathetic nervous system takes over and acts like a brake, slowing the heart rate[8] and respiration back down. Most pathways in the parasympathetic nervous system travel through two nerves, which together are called the vagus nerve. These nerves travel from the brain stem through the body and send information to the brain from all the internal organs. When the vagus nerve is activated, the brain gets the signal that it is time to calm down and the natural "rest and digest" and "restore and repair" functions of the body are triggered into action. The body calms down and the ability to think rationally returns.[9]

This is all part of the complex way God designed our bodies to be able to react quickly and efficiently in the face of danger. It's a wonderful system to have when there's a bear suddenly in your path and you need to act quickly. It's not so helpful, however, when it is triggered by things that aren't actually dangerous.

Because we live in a fallen world with imperfect bodies that are no longer perfectly integrated as God first designed, but rather "dis-intigrated"[10] as a result of sin and death, our bodies are prone to dysregulation. As a result, the natural processes that help regulate anxiety can often get out of balance. Sometimes the sympathetic nervous system is triggered by things that aren't really valid threats. Our worries and fears are not always grounded in actual danger, and our stress response can overreact and prepare for fight or flight when no real threat is present. Sometimes the sympathetic nervous system can remain highly active much longer than necessary instead of returning to baseline, while the parasympathetic nervous system is underactive and unable to effectively "put the brakes" on feelings of anxiety.

Balancing the sympathetic and parasympathetic systems is an important step to regulating our emotions. This is where intentional breathing can help. Breathing is one way to calm the physical symptoms of anxiety and restore alignment within the nervous system.

BREATHING: THE BRIDGE BETWEEN THE BRAIN AND THE BODY

"Breathing is the bridge between the brain and the body." I first heard these words from psychiatrist Dr. John Bocock, in our first visit with him. Our daughter had been diagnosed about a year earlier with Generalized Anxiety Disorder and suffered from severe and frequent panic attacks, and his first bit of professional advice was centered on breathing and the power of the breath, especially as it relates to managing anxiety.

Just as emotions like worry and fear can trigger the body's stress response, what we experience physically in the body can affect our emotions. Because of this, we can often begin to quiet our worries and calm the symptoms of anxiety simply by controlling one critical body function: breathing.

Breathing is one of the few body processes that can be regulated both consciously and unconsciously.[11] We cannot intentionally lower our heart rate or willfully regulate our blood pressure, but we can control our breathing. We can intentionally make our breaths slow and deep, or rapid and shallow.

Breathing gives us a direct connection to the vagus nerve in our parasympathetic nervous system. Changing our breathing can directly affect the signals being sent from the vagus nerve to the brain.

Dr. Curt Thompson writes, "By controlling our breath, we can willfully influence the brain and the autonomic nervous system and literally change our mind-body state. By changing the pattern of our breathing, we change the pattern of the information being sent to the brain. In other words, how often, how fast, and how much you inflate your lungs directly affects the brain and how it operates."[12]

Breathing gives us a way to hack into our own brain and nervous system!

SMELL THE FLOWERS; BLOW OUT THE CANDLES

Deep breathing exercises—also called breathwork—take practice over time to become effective.

If you do not have any experience with breathwork, I've included three common diaphragmatic breathing techniques that have been shown to activate the vagus nerve. Instructions are on page 32 and sample techniques are on page 35.

Breathwork is focused on intentional breathing. It is important to inhale slowly and deeply through the nose and exhale slowly and completely through the mouth. A common phrase that helps us remember this is: "Smell the flowers and blow out the candles." As you "smell the flowers," breathe in deeply and focus on filling your diaphragm completely, letting your stomach fully expand. Most of us typically breathe by expanding the chest, so diaphragmatic breathing may take some practice. Then as you exhale, envision you are blowing out the candles on a large birthday cake. Take your time as you expand the length of your exhale to blow out all those candles.

When done regularly, this kind of breathwork has many proven benefits, including reducing stress and assisting with pain management.[13] Numerous studies have shown that breathwork is also effective against anxiety, depression, and insomnia;[14] it has also been shown to reduce blood pressure, increase heart rate variability and oxygenation, enhance pulmonary function, and improve cardiorespiratory fitness and respiratory muscle strength.[15]

Breathwork is great. The benefits are undeniable. But breathwork alone is incomplete. It does not address our deepest need.

BREATH PRAYER AS A SPIRITUAL PRACTICE

For centuries people have integrated breathwork into spiritual practices like meditation and mindfulness, connecting the breath to not just the body but also to the mind and soul, making breathwork not just a physical experience but a spiritual one as well. Many of these practices often involve attempting to *empty* the mind or looking *within self* to find peace. These techniques may have some benefits, but mindfulness and meditation that is not centered in Christ and His love for us will not lead to true flourishing—it may help give our bodies a temporary reprieve from the physical symptoms of stress, but we miss out on the deeper connection our souls long to have with Christ.

Christian meditation is about *filling* the mind with the Word of God and looking *to God*, not inside ourselves, for peace.

The one important thing that sets breath prayers apart from mere breathwork and mindfulness is *prayer*.

Prayer is the key that changes everything.

We've already established that breathing is the bridge between the brain and the body.

In a similar way, prayer acts as a bridge between God and His people.

Sin broke the intimate connection we had with God. Christ reestablished that connection through His death and resurrection, making a way for us to know Him, and now we have direct access to Him through prayer.

Prayer is a bridge from our heart to His. It's like our spiritual breath:

- Breath has a rhythm to it, a cadence of inhales and exhales. Prayer has a rhythm too, a cadence of inhaling God's grace and exhaling our fears.

- Breathing can help reset and realign your nervous system. Prayer can help reset and realign your soul.

- Deep breathing can calm the brain and the body. Prayer can calm the mind and the soul.

When we pray, we inhale the truth of God's presence and love, breathing in His goodness and grace—and we exhale the weight of our fears and anxieties, giving God all our worries and wants.

Breathing techniques alone can be helpful, but when you connect it to prayer you have a powerful tool that can bridge the brain, body, mind and soul, especially in times of stress. Breath prayer can help calm your anxiety by connecting you to your Creator and aligning your breath to rhythm of His grace.

Anxiety makes us focus on ourselves and our feelings and the discomfort that those feelings and emotions are causing us. In breath prayer, we reorient our thoughts toward Christ and He becomes the center of our focus, not our feelings.

Breath prayer can be a lifeline in times of anxiety and a doorway into an even deeper prayer life as you intentionally realign your heart with the One who made you and loves you and is always with you.

Anxiety doesn't have to be a road block to your faith.

Unless you're being attacked by a bear or facing an actual threat, anxiety can simply be a signal to slow down, take a deep breath, and pay attention to what you are thinking and feeling in that moment. Anxiety doesn't have to trigger you to spiral into panic, but can instead trigger you to turn to Christ in prayer. So when anxiety begins to press in, take some time to slow down and breathe. Use the breath prayers in this book as guide to pray as you breathe, or pray your own words to God, giving Him your worries and accepting His breath of peace.

There's one God and only one, and one Priest-Mediator between God and us— Jesus, who offered himself in exchange for everyone held captive by sin, to set them all free.

I TIMOTHY 2:5–6 THE MESSAGE

Breathe in deeply. God gives you breath. He will give you everything you need. Things may not feel ok right now, but that's ok. Because God is still with you.

Exhale slowly. No need to rush. God is in control. He knows what He is doing. You are safe and held and loved.

Repeat the breath prayer as many times as you need to until your anxiety eases, your body and brain calm, and your soul and mind come back into alignment with Christ and His love for you.

The more you respond to anxiety this way, the more automatic this response will become. This change doesn't happen overnight, and it will take repeated practice over time to experience more significant results. But as you practice breath prayers, you actually begin to change the neural networks in your brain. In science, they call this neuroplasticity: your brain is a dynamic organ that can literally be changed and reshaped as you learn and grow and experience new things. I like to think of it as a remarkable example of how you are literally being "transformed by the renewing of your mind" (Romans 12:2). God changes us from the inside out as we intentionally and consistently turn to Him.

By turning your thoughts to Truth and reorienting your heart to Christ through prayer, you participate in the work of the Holy Spirit and "let God transform you into a new person by changing the way you think" (Romans 12:2 NLT).

You are created for so much more than an anxious life full of fear and worry—you are called to an abundant life of peace and joy as you are transformed by Christ and your mind is renewed day by day.

Anxiety is not an enemy you need to fight. It is an opportunity to slow down and invite Christ into your struggle, to breathe deep in His presence and let His peace enter into all your broken places. I invite you to practice the breath prayers in this book, and I challenge you to make them a daily habit.

Give it a try for a week, a month, or even three months, and see what effect this practice has on your anxiety. How does it affect the physical symptoms you feel in your body? How does it affect your soul and your relationship with God? Slow down and pay attention for just five minutes every day, even on days when you may not be feeling particularly anxious, and take time to breathe deeply and listen to the voice of God reminding you that you are safe and known and loved and held, today and always.

Breath prayer

BASICS

Breath prayers can be done at anytime and anywhere
you are able to slow down, be still, and breathe.

Breathe in deeply and slowly through your nose. Feel your lungs fill completely.

Focus on filling your lower lungs (your diaphragm) so that your stomach expands while your upper chest remains still.

Breathe out slowly. Empty your lungs fully.

Repeat a few times as you bring your breathing into a slow and steady rhythm.

Inhale: Continue breathing slowly as you pray. Fill your lungs slowly as you say the "inhale" part of the prayer.

Exhale: Empty your lungs slowly as you say the "exhale" part of the prayer.

Meditate on the words as you breathe to the rhythm of the prayer.

how & why THEY WORK

Breath prayers combine deep breathing exercises with prayers of meditation on God's Word. Slow, deep breaths help activate the parasympathetic nervous system, slowing the heart rate and calming the body, while prayer turns the heart toward Christ, focusing the mind on truth and calming the soul.

Repeat the breath prayer, inhaling and exhaling slowly, for at least one minute.

Try to work up to five-minutes.

Breath prayers can be done
at any time and anywhere
you are able to slow down,
be still, and breathe.

breathe

365

three times per day, six breaths per minute, five-minute duration

- Inhale slowly through the nose for **five** seconds
- Exhale slowly through the mouth for **five** seconds
- Repeat for **five** minutes

4–7–8 (THE RELAXING BREATH)

- Inhale slowly through the nose for a count of **four**
- Hold your breath for a count of **seven**
- Exhale completely through your mouth for a count of **eight**
- Repeat the cycle three more times for a total of four breaths

SQUARE BREATHING

(also called "box breathing")

- Inhale slowly through the nose for a count of **four**
- Hold your breath for a count of **four**
- Exhale slowly through the mouth for a count of **four**
- Hold your breath for a count of **four**

"in prayer
we intend to
leave the world
of anxieties
and
enter a world
of wonder."

EUGENE PETERSON
Answering God

Breath Prayer
T H E M E S

Prayers of Trust
Trust God with your life

Prayers of Love
Abide in God's unfailing love

Prayers of Surrender
*Give God your worries
& surrender to His will*

Prayers of Direction
*Turn to God, follow Him
& let Him guide your path*

Prayers of Help
Depend on God to help you

Prayers of Hope
Hold on to hope

Prayers of Presence
Know God is always with you

Prayers of Peace
Experience peace in your soul

Prayers of Strength
Trust God to strengthen you

Prayers of Protection
Rest safely under God's protection

Prayers of Gratitude
*Focus on God's goodness
& give Him thanks*

Prayers of Repentance
*Seek forgiveness & freedom
from the weight of sin*

GOD IS YOUR SHEPHERD

Breathe Deep and Know: *The good Shepherd is with you. You have everything you need.*

One of the most beautiful and comforting pictures of how God loves and cares for us is when He is shown as a shepherd caring for His sheep. Jesus Himself tells us, "I am the good shepherd; I know my own sheep, and they know me" (John 10:14).

A flock of sheep is fully dependent on their shepherd. On their own, domesticated sheep are prone to wander, exposed to danger, unable to right themselves if they fall and they can even have trouble finding their own food or water. But under the care and guidance of a loving shepherd, sheep are led safely to bountiful green pastures, protected from dangerous predators, picked up and steadied when they fall, and guided back to the flock when they are spooked or start to wander away. Sheep can actually recognize their shepherd's face and they know their shepherd's voice. They trust their shepherd and depend on him to provide everything they need.

As your good shepherd, the Lord is lovingly guiding you and providing for you today. No matter your circumstances or the path that this life has you on, the Lord, your shepherd, is with you. You don't have to worry or be afraid. Simply stay with the Shepherd. With Him, you will always have all that you need.

The Lord is my shepherd; I have all that I need.
PSALM 23:1

inhale:

THE LORD IS MY SHEPHERD,

exhale:

I HAVE ALL THAT I NEED.

GOD IS YOUR REFUGE

Breathe Deep and Know: *You are not alone.*
God is with you, to help you and offer refuge,
to give you strength when you are weak.

Are you troubled by anxiety? Do fear and worry press in and paralyze you? What about the sleepless nights when racing thoughts won't still? All of us experience these things from time to time—and more acutely during challenging or stressful seasons of life. But we aren't alone in these battles.

When anxiety presses in and trouble seems to surround you, when you are weak and feeling alone, run to Jesus. Turn to Him. He is a refuge, a safe place, a safe shelter during the storm. He is your strength when you're weak, a steadying hand when you're stumbling in the dark. He is with you—by your side, ready to help you—no matter what trials or troubles you are facing. You don't have to go it alone. So instead of responding to trouble and stress with panic or fear, let those feelings be a signal to turn toward Christ and seek the peace that comes from taking shelter in His presence.

God is our refuge and strength,
a very present help in trouble.

PSALM 46:1 ESV

inhale:
YOU ARE MY
REFUGE AND
STRENGTH,

exhale:
A VERY
PRESENT HELP
IN TROUBLE.

GOD IS YOUR SHIELD

Breathe Deep and Know: *You can rest behind God as your shield, knowing He will help you and protect you.*

A shield's purpose is to protect. It's the first line of defense, a literal barrier between you and the danger that is coming at you, helping to ward off attacks. For an enemy to get to you, they must get through the shield first.

We're good at constructing our own shields, assembling armor around our hearts in an attempt to protect ourselves from the pain and disappointments and worries of this life. But even the strongest shields are imperfect. No shield of our own making will ever be strong enough.

God is your perfect shield and your strength. You don't have to be strong enough because He is. He is there to protect you and to be the strength you need. Are you feeling weary today? Vulnerable to the attacks of life and an onslaught of worry? Let God be your shield. He is stronger than any enemy that threatens you. His shield of protection will hold steady and sure no matter what weapon is wielded against you.

The Lord is my strength and shield. I trust him with all my heart. He helps me, and my heart is filled with joy.

PSALM 28:7

inhale:
You are
my shield

exhale:
I trust you to
help me.

YOU CAN GIVE GOD YOUR BURDENS

Breathe Deep and Know: *You can let go of the burdens you're holding. You can trust God to take care of you.*

Very often, anxiety is directly tied to the burdens and worries we're carrying. You know that feeling, when circumstances are out of your control, uncertainty is pressing in, and the future is unclear. It's so easy to worry and let the weight of that worry weigh you down. It often seems like an instinct that is hard to control, like worry is just an automatic response to stress.

But the truth is, no amount of worry ever does us any good. We may feel like we are taking action when we worry, but worrying has never solved a problem, predicted an outcome, or calmed a heavy heart. In fact, worry often leads to anxiety, which activates our stress response and dysregulates our bodies. And for believers, worry ultimately reflects our doubt in the care and provision of God. Instead, the Bible tells us, "Don't worry about anything; instead, pray about everything. Tell God what you need, and thank him for all he has done (Philippians 4:6).

What burdens are you holding onto today? What do you need to give to God and entrust to His care?

Give your burdens to the Lord, and he will take care of you. He will not permit the godly to slip and fall.

PSALM 55:22

INHALE:

I give my
burdens
to You;

EXHALE:

You will
take Care
of Me.

GOD'S LOVE IS LIMITLESS

Breathe Deep and Know: *There are no limits
to God's love and faithfulness to you.*

Nothing you can do could ever stop God's love for you, and yet we often live as though our problems are bigger than He is. We are afraid and stressed, worried and restless. We may say we believe God and His promises, that His love is higher and greater and stronger than anything, but do we *really*?

Get honest today. What limits have you placed on the love and faithfulness of God?

Is there a diagnosis, a relationship, a stressful situation at work, a rejection or betrayal, a sin or bad choice that you think overshadows His love for you or His faithfulness to you?

Name that thing.

No matter what it is, God is higher and His love is greater than even that. Breathe in the truths of this prayer and rest in His unfailing love today.

----

*For your unfailing love is higher than the heavens.
Your faithfulness reaches to the clouds.*

PSALM 108:4

inhale:

YOUR UNFAILING LOVE

exhale:

IS HIGHER THAN
THE HEAVENS,

inhale:

YOUR FAITHFULNESS

exhale:

REACHES TO
THE CLOUDS.

GOD'S WAY IS BEST

Breathe Deep and Know: *God's way is the best way, the perfect way, because His way is built on His promises—promises that will always prove true.*

Every promise of God proves true. Every. Single. One.

- "I am with you always." (Matthew 28:20)
- "I will not leave you or forsake you." (Deuteronomy31:8)
- "I will give you rest." (Matthew 11:28)
- "I will help you." (Isaiah 41:13)
- "My unfailing love for you will not be shaken." (Isaiah 54:10)
- "No one can take you out of the Father's hand." (John 10:29)

What promise from His Word do you need to remember today? If you're in the middle of a storm, the fear and anxiety you're experiencing can feel greater than the truth; but just because your feelings are overwhelming doesn't mean God's promises are overridden. God doesn't ever say that His way is easy or without difficulty or pain or struggle, but He does tell us that His way is the best way, and we can trust the truth of His promises—they will always prove true .

---

*God's way is perfect. All the L*ORD*'s promises prove true.*
He is a shield for all who look to him for protection.

PSALM 18:30

inhale:

Your way is
perfect;

exhale:

All Your
promises prove
true.

GOD CALMS YOUR ANXIOUS HEART

Breathe Deep and Know: *The same God who stills storms to a whisper can calm your anxious heart.*

Anxiety can feel like a storm inside you. Thick clouds of fear fill your mind as showers of sorrow and suffering spill from your heart and the winds of uncertainty blow in from every side. It's easy to feel tossed on the waves, drowning in a raging sea of worry or pain.

But God is powerful. With a word, He can calm the waves. With a breath, He can still the storms. His presence alone turns thunder to a whisper and crashing waves into hushed silence.

The same God who calms the storms of the sea can calm your heart today. The waves of your circumstances may keep rising, and the thunder of fear may continue to boom, but there can be peace and calm in your soul when you focus on the One who is with you rather than the storm that surrounds you.

What waves are crashing into you today? What thunder is drowning out His voice?

Name the storm you're in; then trust that God has the power to calm it to a whisper. And trust that if He doesn't calm the storm, He will calm *you* through the storm. He's riding those waves with you, right by your side.

Then they cried out to the LORD in their trouble, and he brought them out of their distress. He stilled the storm to a whisper, and the waves of the sea were hushed.

PSALM 107:28-29 CSB

inhale:

YOU STILL THE STORMS TO A WHISPER,

exhale:

YOU HUSH THE WAVES OF THE SEA.

YOU CAN SURRENDER YOUR WORRIES

Breathe Deep and Know: *God cares
about you. Give Him all your worries—
He'll carry them, and He'll carry you.*

When I'm weighed down by the many burdens and worries of life, I often
have to remind myself: *God cares for me. I can give Him my deepest worries, my most irrational fears, my wounds and my doubts. He carries my
cares. And He carries me. He has sustained me till now, and He will sustain
me still—no matter what.*

What cares are you holding onto today? What worries are weighing you
down? What burdens are heavy on your heart? Take a moment to name
them. Write them down. Now, as you pray, lay these worries down—literally, set the words you've written down on the floor in front of you—as
you would lay them at His feet. Surrender them all to God today.

He wants you to give Him your worries because He cares about you.
He already knows the heavy weight that you're carrying and He invites
you to give it all to Him. Let Him carry you and all your worries, too.

---

*Give all your worries and cares
to God, for he cares about you.*

1 PETER 5:7

INHALE:

I give you my worries + cares,

EXHALE:

for You care about me.

YOU CAN REST IN GOD'S GOODNESS

Breathe Deep and Know: *No matter what your anxiety may be telling you, God is good, and your soul can rest in His love.*

Prayer helps us experience the love and acceptance of Christ, reminding us of His goodness and allowing our souls to rest in His love, no matter the circumstances we're in or the anxiety we're feeling.

It can be very difficult, however, to embrace or even fully process God's goodness when your nervous system is dysregulated. In times of heightened anxiety or stress, the sympathetic nervous system goes into overdrive, sending the body into fight, flight, or freeze. In those moments, the feelings of fear and anxiety overpower the feelings of love and acceptance you have in Christ.

This is where breath prayers can help. By slowing your breathing, you can calm the sympathetic nervous system and allow the parasympathetic nervous system to take over. This is the perfect time to begin intentionally shifting your focus away from the fear you're feeling and toward the truth and goodness of God. As you breathe deeply and intentionally, try naming one good thing God has done for you. Focus on His goodness with your breaths. Let your mind fill with gratitude and your soul fill with peace as you focus on God's love and goodness to you.

Let my soul be at rest again, for the Lord *has been good to me.*
PSALM 116:7

inhale:

Let my soul be at rest;

exhale:

You have been good to me.

GOD STRENGTHENS YOU

Breathe Deep and Know: *God is gracious and kind, and He will be your strength through every day.*

With the dawn of each new day comes the gift of renewed hope and strength. As the sun breaks through over the horizon and the darkness of night is pierced with bright rays of its light, so the strength of God can break through our weakness, piercing our distress with bright rays of hope.

You may not feel it right now—you may be weary from a lingering season of sorrow or stress, you may be struggling to hold onto hope in the midst of pain or discouragement, you may be experiencing intense anxiety or fear. But your strength doesn't come from how you're feeling but rather from Who you're trusting.

Pray this breath prayer to God today. Ask Him to be your strength and salvation in the midst of whatever trouble or suffering or stress you're facing. Wait for Him and rest in Him and trust His heart for you today.

Lord, be gracious to us; we long for you. Be our strength every morning, our salvation in time of distress.

ISAIAH 33:2 NIV

inhale:

BE MY STRENGTH
EVERY MORNING

exhale:

AND SAVE ME
IN MY DISTRESS.

GOD IS YOUR HELP

Breathe Deep and Know: *Your help comes from the Lord, the One who made you and loves you more than all of heaven and earth.*

The Creator of the universe—the Giver of life and the Maker of the heavens and all the earth—is the One who is with you, by your side, ready to help you. Is anything too big for Him, too difficult for Him to do? If His breath can create life, if a single word from His mouth can birth stars and planets, surely He is able to help you, no matter what you're facing.

His help may not come in ways you expect. His help may not be in the form of complete physical healing or total relief from suffering—but His help will come. It may come through the compassion and care of people in your life. It may come through medications or therapy. Or it may come as an indescribable inner peace, the kind that only He can give—as He stands with you in the fire, as He walks with you through the wilderness, and as He wraps His arms around you through the storm. Look for the ways God is helping you today. Can you see your Maker's helping hand in your circumstance today?

My help comes from the Lord,
who made heaven and earth.

PSALM 12

INHALE:

My help
Comes from
You,

EXHALE:

Maker of
heaven
and
earth.

GOD'S LOVE IS STEADFAST

Breathe Deep and Know: *Just as nothing can stop the sun from rising or the morning from coming, nothing can stop God's love and mercy for you.*

When we're in the middle of hard things we can't control, we can feel desperate to grasp onto something we can do to make it better. It's as if we think that "pleasing" God by doing enough good things means He'll answer our prayers and do what we want Him to do and take the hard things away.

But that's not how God works. Our actions don't earn God's goodness. God's goodness is always first, before we ever do anything. God *is* good. It's who He is. His love and His faithfulness are not changed by what we do or don't do. The love of God never stops. His goodness and kindness and mercy never end.

It is on the foundation of His steadfast love that we pray for healing, not on any good we do to try to earn it. Trusting His kindness is what allows us to know peace, whether the healing we pray for comes or not. Because whatever comes *is* the kindness of God, and whatever tomorrow may bring, new mercies will always accompany that sunrise.

The steadfast love of the Lord never ceases; his mercies never come to an end; they are new every morning; great is your faithfulness.

LAMENTATIONS 3:22–23 ESV

inhale:
YOUR STEADFAST LOVE NEVER STOPS,
exhale:
YOUR MERCIES NEVER END;
inhale:
THEY ARE NEW EVERY MORNING;
exhale:
GREAT IS YOUR FAITHFULNESS.

MAKE IT A HABIT TO SEEK GOD

Breathe Deep and Know: *God knows what's best for you. Make it a habit to seek Him and ask Him to align your heart with His so that you won't wander away from His will.*

Just as consistent exercise trains the body (builds strength, endurance, flexibility), intentionally seeking God through consistent prayer trains the heart to live in rhythm with Christ and helps you to follow His ways. You can face trials with endurance, pursue dreams in His power, adjust to life's surprises with a flexibility that comes only because of the strength of connection with God. Just as regular deep breathing exercises can help calm your nervous system and regulate the connection between your brain and your body, regular prayer and communication with God can calm your mind as you connect your soul with Christ. Together, breath and prayer can reduce anxiety and bring clarity as you intentionally seek God and follow His ways.

When you create a habit of prayer in your life—when it becomes part of your everyday rhythm—you will train your mind and soul to go to God first, in all things. Seek Him with your whole heart and see how it strengthens you day by day.

With my whole heart I seek you; let me not wander from your commandments!
PSALM 119:10 ESV

inhale:

I SEEK YOU WITH MY
WHOLE HEART,

exhale:

DON'T LET ME
WANDER FROM YOUR
COMMANDS.

GOD KNOWS YOUR NEEDS

Breathe Deep and Know: *God wants to hear from you today. Pour your heart out to Him, tell Him what you need, and then trust Him to provide what's best for you.*

What do you need today? Have you asked God about it yet?

He's inviting you to pray, to talk to Him, to unload your heart and tell Him what you need. He will meet you where you are and provide what He knows is best for you because of His deep love for you.

You may wonder, *if He already knows what I need, then what's the point of praying for it?* Prayer isn't as much for God's sake—to tell Him what He, an omniscient Creator, already knows—but for our sake—to redirect our minds and realign our souls to Him and His will for our lives.

Prayer is not a magic formula and God is not some genie in a bottle waiting to grant all your wishes. Prayer is a bridge that connects your heart to Christ. It helps align you with His heart as you remember the truth that He loves you and He knows what you need. When you fully trust His heart for you, then you can give Him your needs and rest, knowing that He knows the very best way to meet those needs.

"For your Father knows exactly what you need even before you ask him."

MATTHEW 6:8

inhale:
You already
know

exhale:
everything
I need.

YOU ARE CARRIED

Breathe Deep and Know: *He is carrying you. You are held safe in His hands.*

Sometimes we forget that we are held. The darkness of suffering closes in and it's hard to see—hard to see those around us, to see our support systems, to see the gifts and mercies present even in the darkest of times. It feels like we're alone, abandoned, and left to fend for ourselves. Prayer adjusts our eyes to see the truth: in the darkness, His hands are enfolding us; through the unknown, His arms are carrying us.

The God who made you, who knit together every cell and fiber of your being, is the One who sustains you. Right now in this moment, He is holding you. And He will never ever stop—not today, not tomorrow, not on days when hope is hard to hold or the dark is closing in—there will never be day in all of your days when His loving arms aren't carrying you through.

"Even to your old age and gray hairs I am he, I am he who will sustain you. I have made you and I will carry you; I will sustain you and I will rescue you."

ISAIAH 46:40 NIV

inhale:

You made me and sustain me,

exhale:

You carry me all of my days.

GOD'S PRESENCE IS THE MIRACLE

Breathe Deep and Know: *You may not get the miracle you ask for, but you always get the miracle you need: God with you. And that is the greatest miracle of all.*

When our children are suffering, when the diagnosis is devastating, when our hearts are hurting, when grief and sorrow are heavy, when the struggles seem endless, when we need a miracle . . .

We call on Jesus and beg Him to help, to heal, to make all things well again.

But sometimes the days just get harder, the struggles continue, the suffering endures, the pain lingers. And we wonder: *Did God hear me? Do I not have enough faith? Why won't He bring healing? Where is the miracle?*

We pray and plead, but still it seems He doesn't move. Have you ever felt that way? I know I have. For a long time, I didn't understand why God didn't seem to be answering my prayers.

He is a miracle-worker and can do anything. Surely He can work this miracle and do this thing. So why doesn't He? Where is He in those moments, when nothing changes, when the circumstances don't improve?

He is here. *With* you. *With* us. By our sides, holding us close all along. We always get a miracle because we get God with us. God's presence is always the miracle— the one we need most of all.

---

*Have I not commanded you? Be strong and courageous.
Do not be afraid; do not be discouraged, for the L*ORD
your God will be with you wherever you go.

JOSHUA 1:9 NIV

inhale:

MAKE ME STRONG
AND COURAGEOUS.

exhale:

I GIVE YOU
ALL MY FEAR.

inhale:

YOU ARE WITH ME

exhale:

WHEREVER I GO.

YOU CAN TRUST GOD
WHEN YOU'RE AFRAID

Breathe Deep and Know: *Your anxiety doesn't have to bind you in fear, but it can be a signal to turn your heart to Christ and deepen your faith as you trust in Him and not in your fears.*

What symptoms do you experience when you are anxious or afraid?

Some common symptoms include flushed face, shaking hands, rapid breathing, dizziness, muscle pain, a knot or ache in the stomach, heaviness or knot in the chest, tightening in the shoulders, headaches, heart palpitations, and even tears.

Identify your physical symptoms when you are anxious, and let these symptoms be a signal to slow down and pay attention—to breathe deeply and turn your mind to Christ. For five minutes, breathe deeply and slowly, and pray the words of this breath prayer. These deep breaths remind your brain that you are safe, and the prayer reminds your soul that you can trust God during times of fear. Your feelings are real, but they don't always tell the truth. When your body is dysregulated, your feelings, while very real and often unsettling, can't always be trusted. But you can always trust God.

But when I am afraid, I will put my trust in you.

PSALM 56:3

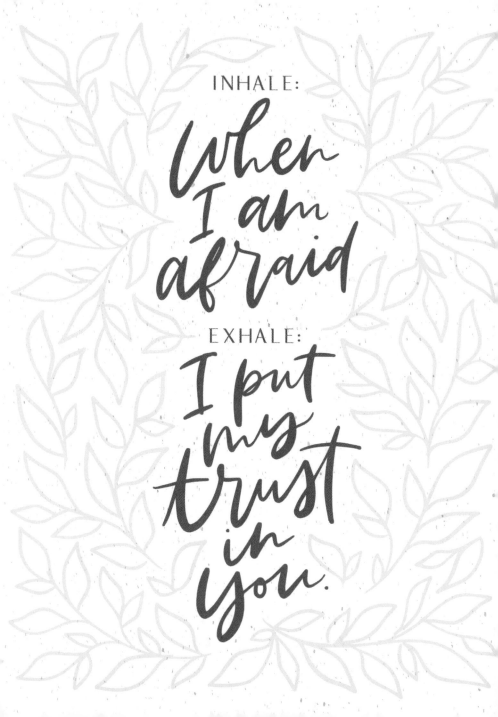

INHALE:

when
I am
afraid

EXHALE:

I put
my
trust
in
you.

GOD IS HOLDING YOUR HAND

Breathe Deep and Know: *You can give the worries you're holding to the One who holds you in His hands. He is there to help you.*

Have you ever been afraid and someone reached over and held your hand? Maybe you were waiting in a doctor's office for some difficult news, or about to get on a ride that was really high and fast, or maybe you were facing a phobia or watching a scary movie or surrounded by a crowd of people or about to walk out onto a stage. There are a lot of things that make us afraid. But there's a special kind of comfort when someone holds your hand, isn't there? It's a simple act of love and support, and sometimes it's just the thing you need to take that next scary step.

God is holding your hand today. Perhaps you feel so afraid that you can't even reach for Him, let alone hold tightly to His outstretched hand. Don't be discouraged. You don't have to be strong enough or brave enough. He is already holding onto you.

Like a father holding his toddler's hand, God's grip on you is not dependent upon your strength, but upon the Father's love. God is holding your hand today. You are safe and loved, and He is here to help you. Give Him your worries and all the things that are making you afraid, and simply take His hand today.

"For I hold you by your right hand—I, the Lord your God. And I say to you, 'Don't be afraid. I am here to help you.'"

ISAIAH 41:13

inhale:

LORD, YOU HOLD MY HAND;

exhale:

YOU ARE HERE TO HELP ME.

IT'S NEVER TOO LATE

Breathe Deep and Know: *It is never too late to start walking in truth.*

Have you ever had a pit in your stomach when you know the choices you've made or the path you're on isn't aligned with God? Sometimes we can work ourselves into a whole mess of worry and anxiety when we know we've made a mistake, sinned in some way, or made poor choices that landed us on a path that we know isn't where God wants us to be.

This kind of anxiety can actually serve a good purpose because it's rooted in conviction that can spur us to turn back to God. If we let it, this kind of anxiety can be a flashing yellow light in our lives, signaling us to slow down and pay attention, perhaps even to turn and go in a different direction.

Is the path you're on right now leading you closer to Christ? Or have you taken a turn somewhere along the way that has you off track? Ask God to teach you His ways so you can walk in the direction of His truth today.

Teach me your way, O Lord, that I may walk in your truth; unite my heart to fear your name.

PSALM 86:11 ESV

inhale:

TEACH ME YOUR WAY,

exhale:

HELP ME WALK IN
YOUR TRUTH.

GOD KNOWS YOUR THOUGHTS

Breathe Deep and Know: *God knows the weight*
of the anxious thoughts you're carrying,
and He invites you to let Him lighten the load.

Imagine for a minute that all of your worries and anxious thoughts are rocks. How many rocks are you holding right now? How heavy is the weight you're carrying? Take an inventory right now and list all the rocks of worry that you're holding onto.

The thing is, if you keep holding onto those worries and anxious thoughts, they will weigh down your soul, and your body and will begin to show signs of that imbalance.

Do you ever feel anxious but don't quite know why? Does your heart race or do your hands tremble? Do you get irritable or have trouble sleeping? When your body begins to show symptoms of anxiety, do you ever slow down and identify your anxious thoughts?

With this prayer, be reminded to regularly ask God to search your heart and reveal your anxious thoughts. Allow Him to bring the source of your anxiety into the light so you can face it and begin letting it go. Let God remove the rocks of worry you're carrying . . . and then let Him carry them for you.

Search me, O God, and know my heart; test me and know
my anxious thoughts. Point out anything in me that offends
you, and lead me along the path of everlasting life.

PSALM 139:23–24

inhale:

Search me and know my heart;

exhale:

I give you all my
anxious thoughts.

GOD IS HEMMING YOU IN

Breathe Deep and Know: *You can choose to be present and grateful in this moment, knowing that God is with you and is hemming you in every step of the way.*

The NIV translates Psalm 139:5 as, "You hem me in behind and before." I love that visual, of God hemming me in, holding me securely, keeping me right in the middle of his presence as He surrounds me all along the way. As a seamstress carefully hems the frayed edges of a garment, God carefully gathers all my frayed edges and tucks me between the threads of His love. His hemming is secure and will never unravel, holding me together every day of my life.

Nothing behind you is beyond God's power to redeem, and nothing ahead of you takes Him by surprise. He knows what has been and what is to come. Sometimes just remembering that truth can ease your worries and remind you to rest in Him.

You may not know what's before you, but you know the One who has already been there. You can't do anything about what's behind you, but you can trust the One who is with you, the One who is going before you and following you, the One who is working all things together for your good and for His glory.

You go before me and follow me. You place your hand of blessing on my head.

PSALM 139:5

INHALE:

You go before me

EXHALE:

and You follow me.

GOD MAKES YOU NEW

Breathe Deep and Know: *There is no sin that is beyond God's willingness and power to forgive. He can purify what sin has tainted, and He can wash the dirt of sin away and make you whiter than snow.*

Before Adam and Eve sinned in the Garden, their bodies functioned in perfect balance, and they enjoyed perfect communion with God. Their bodies, minds, and hearts were whole and without pain, confusion, or sadness. Sin drove a wedge between their souls and the God who made them, and everything changed. Suffering and shame, disconnection and death—all the challenges of the mind and body that we know—became painfully real.

Our bodies still bear the dysregulating and deteriorating effects of sin, and our minds are deeply affected by our own sinful desires. Most significantly, sin separates our souls from an intimate connection with God, which only amplifies the challenges we face. Repentance, therefore, is a crucial step toward realigning our hearts and minds with Christ and welcoming His comfort, peace, and guidance.

Is there a sin in your life that you need to confess to God and repent of today? Do it now. He is ready to meet you where you are with open arms full of forgiveness and grace.

Purify me from my sins, and I will be clean; wash me, and I will be whiter than snow.

PSALM 51:7

inhale:
Purify me
from my sins;

exhale:

wash me
whiter than
snow.

YOU CAN HAVE PEACE AMID THE WAVES

Breathe Deep and Know: *You can experience
God's peace even in the fiercest storms.*

———————————

Think of your heart and mind like a boat. A boat floats because of its buoyancy—the balance between the boat's weight pushing down and the force of the water pushing up. In a storm, as waves crash against the boat, it stays afloat as long as it doesn't take on too much water or tip too far. The boat must maintain balance. A low center of gravity helps keep the boat stable even in high and heavy waves.

The stresses you experience are like the waves that rock the boat of your heart and mind as you navigate the waters of life. And God's peace is like that center of gravity, a balancing, buoyant force holding your little boat steady as it's tossed about on the waves of fear, anxiety, and difficult circumstances. His peace guards your boat from filling with too much water, keeping the waves from capsizing you.

It may seem impossible—a little boat staying afloat in a severe storm. But a boat remains steady not because of the size of the waves but because of its stable center. You can have peace in the middle of your biggest storms when the Person of Christ is at the center of your life. Pray this prayer today and invite Christ into the very center of your life, to protect you and fill you with His peace.

———————————

*And the peace of God, which surpasses all understanding,
will guard your hearts and your minds in Christ Jesus.*
PHILIPPIANS 4:7 ESV

inhale:

GUARD MY HEART AND MIND

exhale:

WITH YOUR
INDESCRIBABLE PEACE.

GOD PROTECTS YOU

Breathe Deep and Know: *God is faithful, and He will strengthen and protect you as you trust in Him.*

Anxiety is as much a physical condition we experience, with symptoms in our bodies, as it is a spiritual battle, with struggles that we experience in our minds and souls. Ephesians 6:12 says, "For we are not fighting against flesh-and-blood enemies, but against evil rulers and authorities of the unseen world, against mighty powers in this dark world, and against evil spirits in the heavenly places."

There is an enemy who wants to keep you bound in the chains of your struggle. And just as we need to be aware of our physical symptoms and care for our body and mind in times of anxiety, we also need to be aware of the "evil one" who would love nothing more than to take us down and keep our spirit bound by fear and shame. This is why we practice both deep breathing *and* prayer in breath prayers. We care for our bodies and minds through deep breathing and mental health care, and we turn to Christ for protection and care of our souls through prayer and time in God's Word.

But the Lord is faithful, and he will strengthen you and protect you from the evil one.
2 THESSALONIANS 3:3 NIV

inhale:

LORD, YOU ARE
FAITHFUL;

exhale:

PROTECT ME FROM
THE EVIL ONE.

YOU CAN TRUST GOD WHEN YOU DON'T UNDERSTAND

Breathe Deep and Know: *The way of God may not always make sense to you, but you can trust Him without fear.*

At the root of my fear is a lack of trust in the heart of God. When the story of my life isn't unfolding the way I thought it would, when a season of suffering lingers longer than I think I can bear, when the news is too bad and bills are too high and tasks are too hard and the pain is too much—when everything looks lost and nothing seems right—it can be hard to see or understand the heart of God. And it's difficult to trust what we don't understand.

But His ways are not at all like ours. There is always more happening than we can see.

Just look at Jesus: the Hope of the world born in the form of a vulnerable infant, the way of salvation forged through significant suffering. What looked like utter death and defeat on the cross was really the way to ultimate life and salvation. What looked like the end was really the beginning of all things being made new.

So that hard thing we don't understand? That pain we fear may break us? It may turn out to be the tool for our rescue. The storm that threatens to drown us may actually be the path to freedom. When we shift the way we see our suffering and trust the heart of God, we can let go of fear and be filled with peace because we know that He is working even if we don't understand.

See, God has come to save me. I will trust in him and not be afraid.
The Lord God *is my strength and my song; he has given me victory.*
ISAIAH 12:2

inhale:

You are my salvation

exhale:

I will trust You
and not be afraid.

NOTHING CAN SEPARATE
YOU FROM GOD'S LOVE

Breathe Deep and Know: *No matter how you feel, you can be confident in the truth that you are truly and deeply loved by God and absolutely nothing can separate you from His love.*

The love of God is unrelenting and unending, passionate and persistent, faithful and enduring.

Even when you are the most unlovable, He still loves you.

Even when you don't feel His love, it is still there, as strong as ever.

Your afflictions can't stop His affection. Your problems can't stop His promises. Your failures can't stop His faithfulness. Your questions can't stop His compassion. Your pain can't stop His plan. Your mess can't stop His mercy.

And absolutely NOTHING—nothing you say, nothing you do, nothing you feel, nothing in heaven or on earth, not even life or death—can separate you from His love.

You are safe and secure and fully and completely loved. You can take a deep breath today and let your worries fade into His loving arms. He's got you.

For I am convinced that neither death nor life, neither angels nor demons, neither the present nor the future, nor any powers, neither height nor depth, nor anything else in all creation, will be able to separate us from the love of God that is in Christ Jesus our Lord.

ROMANS 8:38–39 NIV

INHALE:

Nothing Can Separate me

EXHALE:

from Your Love.

STRENGTH IN YOUR WEAKNESS

Breathe Deep and Know: *Your weakness is not a failure but is instead the fertile ground for God's strength to flourish in your life.*

Our culture doesn't celebrate weakness. Strength, ability, and achievement are the goals of this world. Independence and self-sufficiency are the qualities of high praise. Those perceived to be weak are overlooked and undervalued. They are often stepped over and pushed to the side.

But the kingdom of God is upside down. The last will be first. The weak are strong. The poor inherit the earth.

Your weakness is an opportunity for God's strength to shine in your life. His power works best when we are weak. If we had the strength to get through our suffering on our own, we wouldn't need God. Our weakness is what drives us to dependence on Him, which is where we find true strength.

So turn to God. Release the mistaken belief that you should be able to handle it all on your own, that you should be strong enough or brave enough to endure. God is already strong enough, and He is all you really need.

Each time he said, "My grace is all you need. My power works best in weakness." So now I am glad to boast about my weaknesses, so that the power of Christ can work through me. That's why I take pleasure in my weaknesses, and in the insults, hardships, persecutions, and troubles that I suffer for Christ. For when I am weak, then I am strong.

2 CORINTHIANS 12:9–10

inhale:
YOUR GRACE
IS ALL I NEED;

exhale:
YOUR POWER WORKS
BEST IN MY WEAKNESS.

inhale:
WHEN I AM WEAK,

exhale:
THEN I AM STRONG

GOD CAN HANDLE YOUR DOUBTS

Breathe Deep and Know: *God can handle your doubts. He can calm the waves of unbelief in your soul.*

Trust and doubt are opposing waves that seem to constantly rock the ship of my soul, especially in the darkest storms, when it's difficult to see through the pelting rain and pummeling winds.

I am tossed between what I say I believe and what I feel when I'm afraid. Fear makes me doubt God's goodness. Anxiety makes me question His love. One moment, I say I believe Him and trust Him and want to follow Him, and the next moment I'm knocked off my feet by some hard thing and I wonder if He's really even there like I thought He was.

This prayer is one I pray often. "I believe; help my unbelief!" I have faith, but I'm also afraid. I remember what His Word says, but I also struggle with how I feel.

Do you ever feel the same way? Like what you believe and how you feel don't quite match up? Today, let's take a minute to remind our souls what we believe and ask God to fill in the gaps of our unbelief with His amazing grace.

Immediately the father of the child cried out and said, "I believe; help my unbelief!"

MARK 9:24 ESV

inhale:

Lord, I believe;

exhale:

help my unbelief.

GOD GUIDES YOU

Breathe Deep and Know: *Your future is not a surprise to God. He has already gone before you and He knows what lies ahead. You can trust Him to guide you.*

Is your anxiety ever rooted in a fear of the future? Are you worried about decisions you have to make or unsure of what path to follow? Maybe you're worried about:

- what college to attend
- what job to apply for
- what city to move to
- what relationship to invest in
- what house to buy
- what kind of schooling is best for your kids

These and countless other choices can fill our minds with anxiety and dysregulate our bodies as we worry about making the wrong choice.

This prayer points your heart back to God and reminds you to turn to Him for direction. The more we align our souls with Christ, the more we will be in tune with the peace that comes from following Him, and the more we will recognize whether the steps we're taking are in line with His will for our lives. Ask Him for help today, and keep turning to Him as you walk forward in faith.

Show me the right path, O Lord;
point out the road for me to follow.

PSALM 25:4

inhale:

SHOW ME THE RIGHT PATH;

exhale:

POINT OUT THE ROAD
FOR ME TO FOLLOW.

GOD KEEPS HIS PROMISES

Breathe Deep and Know: *You have a hope that cannot be shaken because God can always be trusted to keep His promises.*

———————

My dad taught me a definition for *hope* that he learned more than forty years ago from the man who led him to Jesus and discipled him as a young Christian, Dr. I. Cecil Beach: "Hope is waiting on the promises of God to take place."

I love that definition and the bigger picture of hope it paints. Too often, the hope we cling to is hope for a desired outcome or a happy ending—for things to work out the way we want them to—and we end up disappointed when those things don't happen or go the way we had "hoped." But true hope isn't rooted in what we think is "good"; it's rooted in *the One who is good.*

We can hold tight to this kind of eternal and unchanging hope without wavering because God Himself never wavers. God will always keep His promises, so we can always have hope as we wait on Him.

———————

Let us hold tightly without wavering to the hope we affirm, for God can be trusted to keep his promise.

HEBREWS 10:23

INHALE:

I hold
tight to
my hope
in You;

EXHALE:

You can be
trusted
to keep your
promise.

GOD LOVES YOU

Breathe Deep and Know: *God is good, and He loves you.*

God's goodness and love for you never ends, never wavers, never changes. His love is faithful and forever. Nothing you do can make God love you any more than He already does, and nothing you do can make Him love you any less. He loves you fully and completely, right where you are.

Sure, there may be days when you *feel* separated from His love, and you may doubt the depth of His love because you don't always experience it the way your soul longs to. Sin and suffering have a way of doing that, of disconnecting us from experiencing the full depth of God's love. But through prayer, even this simple breath prayer, your soul will be turned toward God and reminded that He loves you deeply, that He is with you, and that He hasn't abandoned you, no matter what your feelings may try to tell you.

Focus on His goodness, and look for all the ways He shows His love to you today. Release your fear and embrace His love.

Hallelujah! Give thanks to the Lord, *for he is good! His faithful love endures forever.*

PSALM 106:1

inhale:
Lord,
you are good;

exhale:
You love
endures
forever.

YOU CAN BE STILL

Breathe Deep and Know: *You can hush the hurry and be still because God is God and this life He gave you is a gift. Slow down and enjoy it today.*

It's so easy to get caught up in the pace of the world around us, rushing to the next place without any time to pause and breathe. We keep ourselves busy and stay pretty distracted with activities, plans, commitments, and full schedules. We fill our calendars and over-stuff our to-do lists with tasks that seem to never really end. The pace of it all can make us dizzy, reeling from the spin of this life, from the cycle of days with no real time to rest.

I invite you today to slow down and be still. Take even just five minutes to stop everything, still your body and mind, breathe deeply, and focus on one truth:

God is God. You are not God. I am not God. God is the only God. And He is in control.

The world will not stop if we slow down. As Ann Voskamp says, "Life is *not* an emergency. . . . Life is a gift."[16] Every day of this life is a gift from the One who made us and loves us and wants so much more for us than a life of busy rushing. Be still today and know that He is God.

"Be still, and know that I am God."

PSALM 46:10

inhale:

Still my soul;

exhale:

You are God.

TRADE YOUR WORRY FOR PEACE

Breathe Deep and Know: *When you go to God with your burdens, He can exchange your weariness for rest and your worry for peace.*

How are you resting these days? Is anxiety robbing you of true rest and refreshment?

We can't always control what kind of difficulty enters our lives, how long it will last, or how hard it will get. And that—the not knowing—can cause so much anxiety. It can be nearly impossible to truly rest when your mind is full of worries and fears.

But God does have control. He knows your suffering and every detail of how long it will last and how hard it will get. And He says, "Come to Me." He says to give Him your burdens and He will give you rest, even in the midst of the unknown. Because even though the unknown can cause anxiety and restlessness, it's in being okay with the unknown and trusting God—the One for whom nothing is unknown—that you can actually find the peace and rest your soul so desperately needs.

Inhale His rest and exhale your burdens today. You don't have to bear the weight of trying to control it all or know it all, because you are safe with the One who already does.

Then Jesus said, "Come to me, all of you who are weary and and carry heavy burdens, and I will give you rest."
MATTHEW 11:28

inhale:

I GIVE YOU ALL
MY BURDENS,

exhale:

AND YOU WILL
GIVE ME REST.

YOU CAN TURN YOUR EYES TO GOD

Breathe Deep and Know: *No matter how far you may have drifted or how distracted you have been, God is here to guide you back toward His ways.*

———————

Like the current of a river, a current is always flowing in our lives. If we're not paying careful attention, we'll drift along with the current of this world—culture, busyness, consumption, empty pursuits—and drift in ways we never intended. Before we know it, we may have lost all sense of direction and purpose, uncertain of the truths we once saw so clearly.

Prayer is like a rudder that helps us navigate the current and stay away from the riffles and rapids, away from what the Bible calls "worthless" things that can pull us under, distract us from our purpose, and flood us with anxiety.

And so we keep praying. We keep turning our eyes toward Christ because the current of the world never stops trying to pull us away and turn our attention to other things.

Ask God today to turn your eyes from the things that are not worthy of your attention—things that aren't eternal, that won't last, that pull you off course, that fill you with fear—and toward Him and His ways.

———————

Turn my eyes away from looking at what is worthless, and revive me in Your ways.
PSALM 119:37 NASB

INHALE:

Turn my
eyes from
worthless
things;

EXHALE:

Revive me
in Your
ways.

GOD COVERS YOU

Breathe Deep and Know: *God is covering you in His feathers of faithful love today.*

At first glance, feathers may not seem like all that much protection. They seem soft and rather fragile. But a bird's feathers are remarkably designed to both comfort and protect.

Feathers have a smooth part and a fluffy part. The smooth part acts as a sort of raincoat, protecting against wind and rain, and the fluffy part, the down, insulates and keeps a bird warm. Young birds don't yet have fully developed feathers, so they require the protection of a parent's wings to keep them safe and warm through storms and the cold of the night.

If you've ever watched a bird covering its young with its wings, you'll notice that they can sit unmovable for hours on end, as long as it takes, as long as the storm lasts, as long as the babies need protection. Nothing distracts or deters them. They are immovable, firm, steadfast, fixed in place.

In the same way, God's faithful love and promises are never wavering, always true. You are shielded and protected, safe and warm beneath your Father's wings.

He will cover you with his feathers. He will shelter you with his wings. His faithful promises are your armor and protection.

PSALM 91:4

inhale:
COVER ME WITH YOUR FEATHERS,
exhale:
SHELTER ME WITH YOUR WINGS;
inhale:
YOUR FAITHFUL PROMISES
exhale:
SHIELD ME AND PROTECT ME.

YOU NEED NOT FEAR

Breathe Deep and Know: *God can help you replace fear with power, love, and self-control as you turn to Him and trust Him with your life.*

Have you ever felt out of control when you're afraid or extremely stressed? There's a physiological reason that happens. When your nervous system senses danger, the amygdala (sometimes called the emotional brain) takes over and literally bypasses the frontal lobe (sometimes called the logic brain) in order to prepare your body for fight, flight, or freeze, in a process that psychologist Daniel Goleman first called "amygdala hijacking."[17] Your body reacts automatically, without intentional thought, and the result can often leave you feeling like you have no control over your reactions or behavior in that moment.

The limbic system serves your body well when you're facing an actual threat, like a bear attack for example, but it's not as helpful when the "danger" is merely a stressful situation. These are the times when breath prayers, especially when practiced regularly, can be very helpful. As you slow your breathing, you're telling your nervous system that there is nothing to fear, which allows your amygdala to chill out a bit and lets your logical brain begin to function again.

Pray the words of this prayer, and replace feelings of fear with words of truth.

For God gave us a spirit not of fear but of power and love and self-control.

2 TIMOTHY 1:7 ESV

inhale:

YOU DO NOT GIVE A
SPIRIT OF FEAR,

exhale:

BUT OF POWER
AND LOVE AND
SELF-CONTROL.

GOD KNOWS THE LONGINGS
OF YOUR HEART

Breathe Deep and Know: *God knows your heart,*
and He knows your deepest longings.

What are you longing for today? Maybe it's something you haven't said out loud before, a desire deep in your heart that you've never shared with another soul. God sees your heart and He already knows. Before you utter a single word in prayer, God already knows every longing in your heart. Nothing surprises Him. Even when we don't know how to put these desires into words, when we don't know how or what to pray for, "the Holy Spirit prays for us with groanings that cannot be expressed in words. And the Father who knows all hearts knows what the Spirit is saying, for the Spirit pleads for us believers in harmony with God's own will" (Romans 8:26–27).

Go ahead and really talk to God today—surrender your longings to Him and know that He loves you and is holding you tenderly today.

You know what I long for, Lord; you hear my every sigh.
PSALM 38:9

inhale:

You know what I long for;

exhale:

You hear my every sigh.

GOD GIVES GOOD THINGS

Breathe Deep and Know: *God is good. He is with you and surrounding you with His love.*

If you're feeling a lot of anxiety today, it may be difficult to really believe the words of today's prayer. When your mind is filled with fear and your body is feeling the very real physical effects of anxiety, seeing past the things that are troubling you and focusing on the deeper reality of God's love and tender mercy surrounding you can feel impossible.

Take a few minutes today to list some of the good things in your life. What are you grateful for? Start with naming just one thing. Then try two, and then three. Even small moments of gratitude have a powerful way of reconnecting us with the goodness of God that surrounds us.

The hard and scary things may still be there, but so is God. And His goodness pierces through even the darkest of darkness.

He redeems me from death and crowns me with love and tender mercies. He fills my life with good things. My youth is renewed like the eagle's!

PSALM 103:4–5

INHALE:

You surround me with love + mercy;

EXHALE:

You fill my life with good things.

YOU CAN FIGHT DOUBTS WITH TRUTH

Breathe Deep and Know: *You fight doubts when you remind your soul of the truth: The Lord is God; He made you and you are His.*

Speaking truth to your soul helps chase away doubts.

- Doubting your worth? Remind your soul that God made you and He adores you. (Psalm 139:13; Zephaniah 3:17)
- Doubting where you belong? Remind your soul that you are His and you will always belong to Him and with Him. (Psalm 100:3; Galatians 2:20)
- Doubting the purpose in all of this struggle? Remind your soul that the Lord is God, and you are not. He knows and sees and never ever stops working. (Psalm 86:10; 46:10)
- Doubting your ability to do this hard thing? Remind your soul that you are not alone. God is with you and gives you strength. (Psalm 46:1, Philippians 4:13)
- Doubting whether He loves you? Remind your soul that He is your shepherd and that He cares for you more deeply than you can imagine. (Psalm 23:1; John 10:11)

What truth can you tell your doubts today?

Acknowledge that the LORD is God! He made us, and we are his. We are his people, the sheep of his pasture.

PSALM 100:3

inhale:
Lord, I know
you are God;

exhale:
You made me
and I am
yours.

GOD IS ALWAYS WITH YOU

Breathe Deep and Know: *You don't have to be afraid because God is always with you.*

God doesn't just sit up on the mountain top waiting to meet you after you've made the grueling climb out of your valley of suffering. He isn't found only on *the other side* of the dark valley, where the sun is shining and the shadows are far behind you. God is right there in the valley with you, right there in the deepest depths of your fear, no matter how dark it gets. Whatever your present moment is right now, He is with you in it.

Prayer doesn't promise an immediate path out of the valley of suffering. But what prayer can do is tune your soul to the Presence of God. Psalm 23:4 doesn't say "*if* I walk through the darkest valley"; it says "*when* I walk through the darkest valley." The valleys will come. The darkness will cross our paths. But God promises that He is *with* us through it all, walking alongside us on the journey.

As you pray today, reach out through your darkness and feel for His hand. He's right there walking beside you, and He will never leave your side.

Even when I walk through the darkest valley,
I will not be afraid, for you are close beside me. Your
rod and your staff protect and comfort me.

PSALM 23:4

inhale:

I WILL NOT BE AFRAID,

exhale:

FOR YOU ARE WITH ME.

GOD REJOICES OVER YOU

Breathe Deep and Know: *The depth of God's love and joy over you is incomparable. He rejoices over you today.*

Do you believe that God holds you when you're weary? Do you trust that He loves you when you're afraid? Do you confidently believe that He embraces you when you're broken?

Today, turn your heart to these truths:

God is your warrior and protector, giving you refuge and fighting for you.

He is also a gentle shepherd whose presence never leaves, holding you tenderly when you're hurting, soothing your fears and calming you with His love.

He sings over you, like a mother sings over her child. He loves you with a compassion and tenderness that is unmatched. Let His love calm your fears today. You are so very loved.

For the LORD your God is living among you. He is a mighty savior. He will take delight in you with gladness. With his love, he will calm all your fears. He will rejoice over you with joyful songs.

ZEPHANIAH 3:17

inhale:

WITH YOUR LOVE,

exhale:

YOU CALM ALL MY FEARS;

inhale:

YOU REJOICE OVER ME

exhale:

WITH JOYFUL SONGS.

GOD KEEPS YOU IN PEACE

Breathe Deep and Know: *Peace is not found in denying the dark or hiding your feelings but in turning your thoughts to Christ, no matter your circumstances or emotions.*

We all feel emotions. Fear, shame, sadness, grief, panic, loneliness, anger, and joy are all part of the human experience. And it's okay to feel your feelings. They are part of how God made us. Experiencing emotions is not the problem. It's how we respond to our emotions that can cause us problems. But how do we change how we respond to our emotions? By changing how we focus our thoughts, no matter how we are feeling.

Strong emotions like anxiety tend to make us focus on ourselves and on the discomfort our feelings are causing. Remember Peter, walking on the water toward Jesus (Matthew 14:28–30)? When he took his eyes off Jesus and focused on the waves, he began to sink. In a similar way, when our attention is focused on our emotions and the size of the waves of worry we're feeling, we can quickly lose peace and feel like we are drowning. But if we fix our focus on Christ and His love for us, we will have a better perspective as we work through our feelings, and we can begin to respond to our emotions in a way that draws us closer to Him.

Keep your thoughts on Him today, and you can experience peace no matter the waves that surround you.

You will keep in perfect peace all who trust in you, all whose thoughts are fixed on you!

ISAIAH 26:3

INHALE:

Keep me in perfect peace

EXHALE:

as I keep my thoughts on You.

ALL THINGS ARE
WORKING TOGETHER

Breathe Deep and Know: *More is happening than you can see. Living by faith means trusting that the pieces are all working together, even if you can't see the whole picture yet.*

We can't see all the ways God is working in our lives. We may sometimes feel forgotten, alone, or afraid. But the truth is that we are *never* alone and God *never* stops working. He never leaves us.

We don't know how all the days, all the trials, all the messy, imperfect moments are working together. This day, this season, this struggle are tiny pieces of a much bigger picture. Like pieces of a puzzle, we tend to focus on this one little piece in our hand right now—we mull over it, trying to reshape it or change it to force it to fit or make sense. But when we look only at that one piece, we lose sight of the beautiful bigger picture. This little piece on its own doesn't make much sense right now, but as it locks in with the other pieces, a good and beautiful picture will emerge.

Trust God with the pieces of your life, and have faith that He is working it all together into a beautiful picture of His grace.

For we live by faith, not by sight.
2 CORINTHIANS 5:7 NIV

inhale:

Help me live by faith

exhale:

and not by sight.

YOU CAN BE FILLED WITH JOY

Breathe Deep and Know: *God is the source of hope, and He can fill you with joy and peace as you trust in Him.*

What are you filled with today? Is fear or anxiety filling your mind and heart? Or are you full of joy and peace?

I'm fairly certain we'd all choose being filled with joy and peace over fear and anxiety any day, but it often seems impossible to make that shift on our own. And honestly, it *is* impossible. Willpower alone is not enough to be able to release fear and be filled with joy. We can't always force ourselves to stop feeling anxiety and be filled with peace because often anxiety is as much a physical health condition as it is a mental one. Breathing exercises can help to calm the body and relieve some of the physical effects of fear and anxiety, but breathing alone does not fill us with joy and peace or give us confident hope. Only God can do that.

So breathe deeply. Thank God for tools to address your anxiety. And ask Him to meet you there and to bring joy and peace to your heart today.

I pray that God, the source of hope, will fill you completely with joy and peace because you trust in him. Then you will overflow with confident hope through the power of the Holy Spirit.

ROMANS 15:13

inhale:

GOD OF HOPE,
I TRUST YOU;

exhale:

FILL ME WITH
JOY AND PEACE.

GOD RESCUES YOU

Breathe Deep and Know: *God already knows where you are today and how you got there. He sees your suffering and He knows exactly what you need.*

In the garden, after Adam and Eve sinned, they hid from God out of fear and shame, and God asked them, "Where are you?" God didn't ask this because He didn't already know where they were or what they had done. He didn't ask for his own sake but for theirs. And He asks that same question of us even now.

Where are you? How are you, really?

Have you paid attention lately to your physical and spiritual reality? How is your body feeling? Are any symptoms telling you to slow down and pay attention? How is your soul and your relationship with God? Do you need to confess anything? Is anything causing dysregulation in your body or your soul?

Where are you today?

God already knows. And He knows how to help you, how to rescue you. Do you trust Him enough to come out of hiding and let Him care for you? Unload your burdens to Him today, and let Him cover you with His love.

Look upon my suffering and rescue me,
for I have not forgotten your instructions.

PSALM 119:153

inhale:

You see
my suffering.

exhale:

Rescue me.

YOU ARE KNOWN

Breathe Deep and Know: *Your soul's deepest longing—to know God and be known by God—is fulfilled through Christ.*

We were created for a relationship with God—to know Him and to be known by Him. This relationship is what changes everything. It's what breathes new life into our souls, what gives true peace, what begins the process of Him making all things new in our lives.

When we come to God through faith in Jesus, we get to reconnect with the One who made us and loves us, the One who stretched out His nail-pierced hands to bridge the gap between heaven and earth and mend what was broken in our relationship with Him. As we experience the love of Christ in salvation, our souls long for more and more of Him. He is our living water, the source of true life and peace. He sustains and refreshes us.

When you're feeling afraid or anxious, your mind may be so desperate for relief that you forget where to find what you really need. Pray this prayer as you turn your soul toward its truest and deepest longing: God Himself.

As the deer longs for streams of water,
so I long for you, O God.

PSALM 42:1

inhale:

AS A DEER LONGS FOR WATER,

exhale:

I LONG FOR YOU, GOD.

GOD HAS A PLAN FOR YOU

Breathe Deep and Know: *God has a plan for you. You can trust Him.*

Every day, I have a choice:

- I can trust my own plans, or I can trust His promises.
- I can lean into my own feelings, or I can lean into His faithfulness.
- I can walk in my own way, or I can follow Him and go His way.
- I can worry about how the future will unfold, or I can rest in the One who is unfolding the future.
- I can hold tight to my plans, or I can surrender those plans and simply hold His hand and trust that His plans are far better than mine.

I don't know what the days ahead hold. But God does. And He says that His plans for me are good and full of hope.

As you pray the words of this breath prayer, do you really believe what they say? What would it look like if you lived as if God has plan for you, as if you truly trusted the hope and the future He has for you?

"For I know the plans I have for you," declares the Lord, *"plans to prosper you and not to harm you, plans to give you hope and a future."*
JEREMIAH 29:11 NIV

INHALE:

I trust the plans you have for me;

EXHALE:

You give me hope and a future.

YOU CAN TURN YOUR THOUGHTS

Breathe Deep and Know: *You can renew your mind by training your thoughts to focus on the things of God.*

You may have heard a saying along the lines of, "Where you look is where you'll go." The idea is that where you place your focus determines your direction.

What you think about matters. What you focus your mind on not only influences your decisions and your direction but can also impact your brain and nervous system. Repeating an action over and over is how the brain makes stronger connections. This is why it can be difficult to break negative thought patterns or automatic responses in times of stress. But it's also why we can have hope, because redirecting your thought patterns can actually change your brain. In a pretty miraculous way, as you turn your thoughts away from sin, worry, or fear and intentionally focus your mind on what is true, noble, and worthy of praise, your brain can actually create *new* neural pathways. The more you repeat the same action—the more you practice turning your thoughts— the deeper those neural pathways become.

When you begin to feel the symptoms of anxiety in your body, use that as a cue to turn your thoughts to something true. When you feel fear creeping into your day, turn your thoughts to what is lovely. When you're tempted by sin, redirect your thoughts to what is right and pure. Train your brain to turn your thoughts to things of God. The more you do it, the easier it will become. In this way, you participate in the work of rewiring your brain and being "transformed by the renewing of your mind" (Romans 12:2).

Finally, brothers and sisters, whatever is true, whatever is noble, whatever is right, whatever is pure, whatever is lovely, whatever is admirable—if anything is excellent or praiseworthy—think about such things.

PHILIPPIANS 4:8 NIV

inhale:

Lord, turn my
thoughts

exhale:

to what is _____

choose one (or more) to focus on in prayer:
true, noble, right, pure, lovely, admirable, excellent, worthy of praise

YOU CAN TRUST GOD IN SUFFERING

Breathe Deep and Know: *You can trust God, even in your suffering.*

Are you suffering in some way today? Is there a pain, hurt, or illness you want God to heal? We pray for healing because God is the great Healer, and we pray for miracles because God is the God of miracles—and it is good to pray for these things.

But sometimes the hurt doesn't heal on this side of eternity. Sometimes pain endures and the suffering is long and the struggle lingers. Those who live with chronic pain or mental health conditions know this well. But that doesn't mean God didn't hear our prayers or that we don't have enough faith.

The truth is, God doesn't always remove the cup of suffering. He didn't take it away from even His own perfect and beloved Son. And although we may not fully understand His ways or His will, we can always trust His heart and rest in His wisdom.

When we pray for God's will to be done, as Tim Keller writes, "It is to say, 'Here's what I need—but you know best.' It is to leave all our needs and desires in his hands in a way that is possible only through prayer. That transaction brings a comfort and rest that nothing else can bring."[18]

"Father, if you are willing, please take this cup of suffering away from me. Yet I want your will to be done, not mine."

LUKE 22:42

inhale:

FATHER, IF YOU
ARE WILLING

exhale:

TAKE THIS SUFFERING
FROM ME

inhale:

YET, NOT MY WILL

exhale:

BUT YOURS BE DONE.

GOD'S MERCY FOLLOWS YOU

Breathe Deep and Know: *Whatever lies in front of you, God's mercy and goodness is following you, chasing you, always pursuing you—all the days of your life.*

If you've ever walked through some dark and difficult days, you know how they can seem to drag on endlessly. When you're in the middle of hard times, it's sometimes hard to remember that these days will not last forever, to remember that goodness and tender mercies are still always coming. The truth is, even when you can't see it or feel it, God's mercy is following you, hedging you in, all the days of your life. You can be sure that grace upon grace will be poured out on these dark and difficult days until something new breaks through the hard ground of this current suffering and light floods the dark places and chases away the terrifying shadows— until all you can see is His goodness and mercy filling your days.

So how do you see His goodness when it's hard to see anything good at all? You look for it. You notice the small ways God's grace and mercy is filling your days. That smile from a friend, that soft blanket on your skin, that warm cup of coffee or that tiny flower on your path. Look for God's goodness today. Focus on His mercy. It's never very far away.

Surely goodness and mercy shall follow me all the days of my life, and I shall dwell in the house of the Lord *forever.*

PSALM 23:6 ESV

INHALE:

Your goodness and mercy follow me

EXHALE:

all the days of my life.

GOD STEADIES YOUR STEPS

Breathe Deep and Know: *Sin causes us to stumble, but God can steady your steps.*

Because of the fall, we are born with a natural lean toward sin. Instead of a steady and upright gait through life, we walk with a tilt that makes us tumble and stumble and trip over our own feet, often causing us to veer off the path that God intended for us, and before we know it we can find ourselves lost in a forest of fear and shame.

Prayer helps right our wayward lean by drawing us closer to God and redirecting our souls toward the path of His love and forgiveness. When we draw close to God in prayer, He steadies our steps as we invite Christ to forgive our sin and lead us back toward His perfect ways. The fallen lean that once led us away from God is now transformed into a surrendered lean toward Him. As we lean on Christ and His promises, we can trust Him to keep us from falling.

Do you feel like you're stumbling a bit today? Turn toward God and trust His promises to steady your steps.

Make my steps steady through your promise;
don't let any sin dominate me.
PSALM 119:133 CSB

inhale:

STEADY MY STEPS
THROUGH YOUR PROMISE;

exhale:

LET NO SIN RULE OVER ME.

GOD IS GOD

Breathe Deep and Know: *God handle all the unknowns. There are no better hands in which to trust your future.*

Sometimes I just need to remember this simple truth: God is God, and I am not.

Oh, how I love to try to try to control every detail in my life. I plan and schedule and make lists for everything. I anticipate what might happen and then rehearse how I will react. I try to orchestrate my days so there is minimum risk for stress and anxiety. But deep down, I know that any control I think I have is just an illusion. Although I use control to try to manage my anxiety, in reality the desire for control actually causes the very anxiety I am trying to avoid.

God is God. I am not. It's okay not to worry about every little thing, to leave our cares in God's capable hands. Our worrying doesn't ensure that bad things won't happen; it just robs us of joy in the present moment. Let God be God . . . and rest in His goodness today.

For you are great and perform wonderful deeds. You alone are God.

PSALM 86:10

inhale:

YOU ARE GREAT
AND DO WONDERFUL
THINGS;

exhale:

YOU ALONE ARE GOD.

YOU ARE PERFECTLY LOVED

Breathe Deep and Know: *You are perfectly and completely loved by God. There is nothing to fear.*

How confident are you in God's constant and never-ending love for you? Do your feelings or circumstances ever cause you to doubt His love? Are you afraid that some situation or event could cause God to stop loving you?

We sometimes feel separated from God's love because sin separates our soul from a close and intimate connection with Him. This can lead to doubting His love because we aren't feeling His love the way we long to.

But love is so much more than a feeling. The love of God for us is a truth and a promise. Prayer allows us reconnect with God and be reminded of these truths that He loves us and is with us and that His love and His presence haven't gone anywhere—no matter what our feelings may be saying. And when we are rooted and confident in His love, no fear can shake it. His perfect love casts out fear.

There is no fear in love, but perfect love casts out fear. For fear has to do with punishment, and whoever fears has not been perfected in love.

1 JOHN 4:18 ESV

inhale:

There is no fear

exhale:

in Your love.

GOD IS NEAR WHEN YOU CALL

Breathe Deep and Know: *God is near when you call on Him.*

When you call on God, He is near to you. He comes close to you, right beside you, and He stays by your side.

Although He is there, you may not always *feel* His presence. Sometimes our fear and anxiety overpower everything, and we feel alone and abandoned in those moments. But the truth and the promise we can cling to is that no matter what emotions we might be feeling, *God is near when we call on Him.* There is no limit to His presence, no qualifications are required to call on His name. He's not just near to some people some of the time; He promises that He is near to *all* who call on him: "Come near to God and he will come near to you" (James 4:8).

Your heart may be swirling with fear or worry today. It's okay. You are not alone. Breathe deeply and rest in His unwavering presence.

The Lord is near to all who call on him,
to all who call on him in truth.

PSALM 145:18 ESV

inhale:
Lord,
you are near

exhale:
to all who
call on You.

YOU CAN DO HARD THINGS

Breathe Deep and Know: *God will give you the strength you need to do hard things.*

You can do hard things—not because you're strong enough but because God is.

Popular memes and motivational quotes might tell you that you have the strength within you to do anything you set your mind to, that everything you need is already inside you, that if you just believe in yourself, you can do anything. But the truth is, your strength is finite. It has an end. And some hard things in life really are too hard to face in your own strength.

Real strength, enduring strength, does not come from within. It comes from the Source of strength Himself, the One who made us, the One who gives life and breath and power to all things. Believing in yourself can't compare to the strength that comes from believing in Him.

Release the hold you have on your life. Relax your muscles, loosen your grip, and allow the strength of God to sustain you. You don't have to be strong enough because *He is strong enough.* You don't need to have all the answers because *He is the ultimate answer.* You can walk this hard road because *He is making a way through.*

I can do all things through him who strengthens me.
PHILIPPIANS 4:13 ESV

INHALE:

I can do all things

EXHALE:

through Christ who gives me strength.

NOTHING IS IMPOSSIBLE WITH GOD

Breathe Deep and Know: *God is with you,*
and nothing is impossible with Him.

What impossible thing are you facing today? What seems too hard, too big, too much for you to manage? Perhaps your impossible thing is a conflict, a betrayal, a decision, a diagnosis, a task, or a situation that you just can't see the way through. Maybe your impossible thing is your anxiety—maybe it feels like it will never get better, like you'll never experience relief from its impact in your life. And maybe this impossible thing you're facing actually *is* impossible, humanly speaking.

Chances are, your body is carrying the stress of that impossible thing. Your nervous system may be struggling to find balance because your mind is overwhelmed. You likely *feel* the physical burden of the impossible things in your life.

But God is bigger than even the most impossible impossibilities and bigger than the overwhelm you are feeling in your body and spirit. With God, all things are possible. Give Him your impossible thing, and allow Him to transform you by renewing your mind as you focus on His presence with you instead of on that impossible thing in front of you.

Jesus looked at them and said, "With man this is impossible,
but not with God; all things are possible with God."

MARK 10:27 NIV

inhale:

With man
this is impossible;

exhale:

but with You,
all things are possible.

GOD WANTS TO BIND
UP YOUR WOUNDS

Breathe Deep and Know: *God longs to heal what's broken and bind up your wounds with His healing grace.*

Sometimes anxiety is rooted in hurt or trauma we've experienced. Trauma is actually a significant factor with many mental health conditions, including anxiety disorders. Take some time today to get really honest with God about your pain and your past. Is there trauma you haven't acknowledged and healed from? Does hurt still linger from heartbreak, betrayal, abuse, or abandonment? God loves you, and He wants to bind up those wounds that are weighing you down.

Let the love of Jesus be a balm over all your broken places. Allow Him to mercifully bind up all your wounds. He can do that through a miracle, or He may work through the people He has put in your life, through therapy, or even through medical intervention. Some hurts are deep, and trauma often requires help from professionals. And that is okay. There is no shame in asking for help. In fact, a new strength comes when you reach out and begin the process of healing. God will meet you there.

He heals the brokenhearted and binds up their wounds.

PSALM 147:3 ESV

inhale:

YOU HEAL THE BROKENHEARTED

exhale:

AND BIND UP THEIR WOUNDS.

YOU CAN LET GO OF CONTROL

Breathe Deep and Know: *You can let go of your grip of control and rest within God's fortress of love.*

I'm really good at making plans and then letting God know what I think is best and how I think things should work out. I like to take the lead, to be in control, to micromanage every detail. My desire for control often manifests as perfectionism, with endless lists and goals and super high expectations. I often think control can ensure my security, keeping my life safe and predictable and on the path I have carved out. But control is an illusion, and perfectionism is a prison.

The truth is, life is unpredictable and full of change. We were never meant to control everything but to trust in God's control. God is constant and His Word never changes. Unlike the weak and unsteady walls of perfectionism and control, God is a true rock and fortress, a strong and sure protection no matter what comes. Leaning into His wisdom to lead and guide us in our lives frees us from the chains of anxiety and knocks down the walls of control.

Since you are my rock and my fortress,
for the sake of your name lead and guide me.
PSALM 31:3 NIV

inhale:

YOU ARE MY ROCK AND MY FORTRESS,

exhale:

I TRUST YOU TO LEAD AND GUIDE ME.

GOD LIGHTS YOUR PATH

Breathe Deep and Know: *No matter how dark the path ahead of you, God can light it up and lead you through.*

Is the path ahead of you unclear? Are you worried about a big decision? Unsure of what your next step should be? Are you anxious about where the path of your life is leading?

Fear activates our fight, flight, or freeze response. Sometimes our fears can keep us from moving forward. We become frozen in uncertainty, paralyzed by anxiety. Sometimes fear can scare us into running ahead without even thinking about the direction we're going. Or we might run in the opposite direction to get past the discomfort as quickly as possible.

Take some time today to give your uncertainty to God. Open the Bible and ask God for wisdom as you take the next step. Let the light of His Word guide your feet. Whether you are tempted to flee from a decision, run ahead without thinking, or you're frozen in fear and unsure of what to do, try slowing down and taking just one small step today. Take a single step of faith, trusting that His Word will light your path one step at a time.

You light a lamp for me. The LORD,
my God, lights up my darkness.

PSALM 18:28

inhale:

Your word is a lamp to my feet;

exhale:

You light up my darkness.

YOU ARE CREATED BY GOD

Breathe Deep and Know: *God made you in a wonderfully integrated way.*

God made you. He made every part of you, including your emotions. Emotions are part of the system that helps us process the sensory input around us every day. They are not an enemy you must fight; they are a signal to pay attention.

Although sometimes it may feel this way, anxiety is not just "all in your head." Notice what happens in your body the next time you feel anxious. Do you start breathing more rapidly? Does your heart begin to race? Do you feel flushed or sweaty or shaky? These physical symptoms are not a coincidence. They are part of the way God intentionally wired you. Stress and feelings of anxiety are cues from our body that something is out of alignment. They are signals that we need to slow down and realign our hearts to Christ and remember the truths of His Word.

Pay attention to how your body processes emotions. It can help you begin to notice cues when it's time to slow down, breathe deep, and refocus—to turn your attention to Christ and tune your heart to His.

For you created my inmost being; you knit me together in my mother's womb. I praise you because I am fearfully and wonderfully made; your works are wonderful, I know that full well.

PSALM 139:13–14 NIV

INHALE:

You created my inmost being;

EXHALE:

I am fearfully & wonderfully made.

GOD GIVES STRENGTH IN THE WAITING

Breathe Deep and Know: *God is growing your strength and courage as you wait on Him.*

What are you waiting for today?

A job? A relationship? An answer to prayer?

Are you waiting for healing? for change? for some kind of rescue?

Are you waiting for the pain to diminish or the storm to lift or the situation you're in to get easier?

We spend a lot of our lives in seasons of waiting. Waiting is hard. Sometimes it seems like it will never end. We get impatient and just want things to work out already. But miracles happen in the waiting. Time spent waiting is never wasted. God is always working, always forming us and transforming us as we wait. And as we often see only in hindsight, some things grow best in the patient seasons of pausing and waiting.

If you're waiting today, ask God to give your heart courage and strengthen your soul as you wait patiently for Him.

Wait for the LORD; be strong, and let your heart take courage; wait for the LORD!

PSALM 27:14 ESV

inhale:

I WILL WAIT
FOR YOU, LORD,

exhale:

GIVE ME STRENGTH
AND COURAGE.

YOU CAN HAVE PEACE AMID SUFFERING

Breathe Deep and Know: *Suffering is part of life,
but we can have courage and peace to walk
through that suffering as we trust in the One
who has already given us ultimate victory.*

Sometimes we get this idea that if only we had more faith or if we just prayed enough or in the right way, all our suffering would go away, our sickness would be healed, and we wouldn't struggle anymore. But God never promised this. In fact, Jesus said that we *will* have suffering; we *will* have trouble. What He promises isn't freedom *from* suffering but His presence and peace *in the midst* of it. We can have ultimate peace because He has already ultimately conquered the world.

The reality is that we may not experience full healing this side of eternity, but we can still have peace that comes only from putting our full trust in Him, knowing that He is writing a good story that is bigger than our current struggles, that He has woven His breath through every moment of our lives, that He is with us and loves us no matter what worries or anxieties may fill our minds. He is a good, good Father. He is with us in our ache, and He wraps our worries in His abiding love.

"*I have told you all this so that you may have peace in me.
Here on earth you will have many trials and sorrows.
But take heart, because I have overcome the world.*"

JOHN 16:33

inhale:

I have peace in You;

exhale:

You have
conquered the world!

GOD HOLDS YOUR DAYS
AND YOUR NIGHTS

Breathe Deep and Know: *God holds your days and your nights in His kind and gentle hands.*

The sun and the moon, the light and the dark, the sunrise and the sunset, the clear skies and the storm clouds—it all belongs to God. He is in control of every rotation of the earth, every revolution around the sun, every season and shooting star. He made them all.

And just as He holds all of creation in His hands, orchestrating the movements of the universe in a delicate and beautiful balance, He is holding you through all your brightest days and the darkest nights, orchestrating your life into a glorious display of His goodness and grace.

It may not be easy to see this when we're walking through those dark seasons and it's hard to make sense of all the shadows, but God is just as present and in control there in the dark as He is in the light of day. He knows what He is doing, and you can trust Him.

As you pray this prayer, be reminded of the One who holds both your days and nights in His hands, the One who is holding you through every moment in life. He is not letting go. You can breathe in peace.

Both day and night belong to you;
you made the starlight and the sun.

PSALM 74:16

inhale:

BOTH DAY AND NIGHT

exhale:

BELONG TO YOU.

GOD WON'T TURN AWAY

Breathe Deep and Know: *It doesn't matter how far you've run away, how long you've been gone, or how lost you've become, God promises that He will not turn away if you return to Him. He loves you and He is calling for you to turn to Him today.*

Every day we are turning. We are always either turning toward Jesus or turning away from Him. There is really no in between.

In order to follow Christ, we have to turn to Him, to focus on Him. If we let our eyes wander, much like what happens when driving a car, we will start to veer and turn in whatever direction we're looking.

Set your eyes on Christ today.

And if you lose focus, if your eyes wander and you begin to worry, if you begin to drift or drown or stray away, rest in this glorious hope: you can turn back toward Him again, and He will always be right there, ready to steady you.

Don't allow your fear or worries to keep you from turning to God. He already knows all your fears, and He loves you. He wants to help you. He wants to hold you. He wants to rescue you. He is calling for you to turn to Him today.

What's one small step you can take today to turn toward God?

For the Lord your God is gracious and merciful and will not turn away his face from you, if you return to him.
2 CHRONICLES 30:9 ESV

inhale:

YOU ARE GRACIOUS
AND MERCIFUL,

exhale:

YOU WON'T TURN AWAY
WHEN I TURN TO YOU.

GOD'S WORD IS YOUR HOPE

Breathe Deep and Know: *God's Word
is your source of hope.*

———

The breath prayers in this book are rooted in Scripture because the Word of God is where lasting hope is found. Scripture is our source of knowledge about God. It's where we learn about His character and promises, about His goodness and grace. His Word is where we are reminded that God is our shield when the enemy's arrows of fear are hurled at us, and He is our shelter when the storms of suffering beat down hard. His Word gives us hope that these dark days are not the end of the story, that the worries of today won't last forever, and that we have a hope that is bigger than our fears.

What is heavy in your life today? Fill your mind with His words, cling to His truth, and let it be your shield and shelter, whatever the day may bring.

———

*You are my shelter and my shield;
I put my hope in your word.*
PSALM 119:114 CSB

inhale:
You are my
shelter and
shield.

exhale:
My hope is in
your word.

YOU CAN TRUST GOD
WITH ALL YOUR HEART

Breathe Deep and Know: *God can be trusted. You can change how you walk through your days, trading worry for peace, when you trust God and lean on Him.*

"Live your truth." "Do what feels right to you." "Follow your heart."

Do these phrases sound familiar? These messages permeate our culture and fill our entertainment and social media feeds every day.

And they sound pretty good—after all, the world sure tells you that going your own way and living your truth are paths to real happiness.

But as followers of Jesus, we know that true joy and peace actually come when we stop leaning on our own understanding—when we let go of our own way, stop clinging to our own truth, stop trusting our own heart—and surrender everything to God and trust Him with our entire life.

What area in your life is causing you anxiety, stress, or worry? Is there a decision you need to make? A sadness or loss that is shadowing your days? Are you truly fully trusting God with that circumstance, or are you only trusting what you can understand? Lean on the wisdom of God, on His eternal truth, to help you find a way forward. You can trust him.

Trust in the LORD with all your heart;
do not depend on your own understanding.

PROVERBS 3:5

INHALE:

I trust you, Lord

EXHALE:

with all my heart.

GOD RENEWS YOUR SPIRIT

Breathe Deep and Know: *God is faithful and forgiving.*

How's your heart today? Are you holding on to sin? Are you struggling to let go of shame or guilt? Is something interfering with your relationship with God?

What about your spirit? Are you anxious or angry? How's your attitude toward the people around you? What kind of spirit would you like to have instead?

Give God whatever you're hanging on to, repent of any sin that is binding you, and let Him work in your heart and your spirit to renew you with His loving grace. He can give you a clean heart and free you from the chains of guilt and shame. The weight you carry will be lifted and you can breathe deeply knowing that He is a faithful and forgiving God, and He invites you to trust Him with your heart and spirit today.

Create in me a clean heart, O God,
and renew a right spirit within me.
PSALM 51:10 ESV

inhale:

Create in me a clean heart,

exhale:

renew a right spirit in me.

GOD'S WORD HELPS YOU REMEMBER

Breathe Deep and Know: *Filling your heart with God's Word is a powerful source of comfort and strength.*

So many of my own struggles start with the act of forgetting what God has already done for me. Ann Voskamp calls it "soul amnesia," and I'm afraid I have a chronic case. I let my emotions cloud out the truth; I let my fears overshadow His promises; I let the lingering storms of my life cause me to doubt His goodness and love. Can you relate?

The remedy for this kind of "soul amnesia" is the intentional act of remembering. We do this by hiding the Word of God in our hearts so we don't forget the truth, so we can honor Him with the way we walk through our days and the way we handle the storms of this life. We memorize Scripture to remember the good He has done and the grace He has given. God's Word helps us remember to get on our knees, to open His Word, to praise His name, to repent of our sins, to look for the good, to count His gifts, and to trust His promises.

The act of memorizing carves strong neural pathways in our brains, making it easier to remember God's promises in times of stress or suffering. If you want to begin hiding God's Word in your heart, the breath prayers in this book may be a great place to start!

I have hidden your word in my heart
that I might not sin against you.

PSALM 119:11

inhale:

FILL MY HEART

exhale:

WITH YOUR WORD.

GOD KNOWS
EVERYTHING ABOUT YOU

Breathe Deep and Know: *God already knows*
everything about you, and He loves you.

Many of us put up walls around our hearts to keep others from truly seeing and knowing us. We worry that if we let someone in, if they see the real us, they won't like what they see , and so we build those walls higher and higher, keeping others at a distance. Shame and insecurity cause us to fear being vulnerable, so we get really good at acting like we have it all together, like we know what we're doing, like we're actually as good and perfect as we wish we were.

But as much as we can allow anxiety and fear lock us away from others, we can't hide from God.

He already knows you—*all* of you. He sees every bit of your heart. He knows the depths of your soul. And guess what? He fully and completely loves and accepts you. There's nothing you can hide from Him. Nothing you've done or can do surprises Him. And because He already knows everything about you, you can trust that He knows what is best for you.

So let God into the deepest parts of your heart today, and trust Him with what makes you most anxious and afraid. You can trust Him with your heart. He loves you.

O Lord, you have examined my heart
and know everything about me.

PSALM 139:1

inhale:

YOU EXAMINE
MY HEART,

exhale:

YOU KNOW
EVERYTHING
ABOUT ME.

GOD IS YOUR STRENGTH

Breathe Deep and Know: *Even if your body is suffering, your soul can be strong. God—the source of your strength—will never leave you. He is yours forever.*

We live in bodies that are riddled with all sorts of afflictions. There are a lot of things we can do to care for our bodies and make them as healthy as possible, but the reality is that every single one of our bodies will fail us at some point.

But even though our bodies may fail and our nervous systems may falter, though we grow weary and tired from the struggles of this life, our souls can remain strong because our strength doesn't come from our circumstances but from God.

Paul wrote in 2 Corinthians 4:16, "Though outwardly we are wasting away, yet inwardly we are being renewed day by day." The state of our soul is not dependent on what is happening in our outer bodies. No matter the illness or disease your body carries, no matter the disorder or diagnosis you've been given, no matter the disability or the difficulty you bear, your soul can flourish and grow and be renewed day by day.

The truth is, I can always have the peace and strength I long for, no matter the state of my body or circumstances, because true peace and strength is found in God, and as the psalmist reminds us: "He is mine forever" (73:26).

My health may fail, and my spirit may grow weak, but God remains the strength of my heart; he is mine forever.

PSALM 73:26

INHALE:

*You are
the strength
of my heart;*

EXHALE:

*You are
mine
forever.*

GOD IS CLOSE WHEN
YOU'RE CRUSHED

Breathe Deep and Know: *You do not suffer alone.*
Jesus is close when you are crushed.

God is not absent in your suffering. You do not suffer alone.

In the depths of the darkness, in the deepest of struggles, at the height of suffering, God is there. And He will not leave, forsake, or abandon you. You can trust Him today, no matter how your heart breaks or how your spirit is crushed. He sees and hears; He knows and cares.

Jesus knows what it is to suffer, to be broken and bruised and despised and rejected. He bears our burdens on his scourged shoulders, and He holds us tenderly in His nail-scarred hands.

Is there a heartache or heartbreak that is weighing on you today? Do you feel alone and broken, longing to be rescued from your pain? Turn to Jesus. Though your spirit may be crushed, He is close. Closer than your next breath.

The Lord is close to the brokenhearted;
he rescues those whose spirits are crushed.
PSALM 34:18

inhale:

You are close to the brokenhearted;

exhale:

You rescue crushed spirits.

GOD SHOWS YOU THE WAY

Breathe Deep and Know: *You may not know the way through this, but God knows the way because He is the Way.*

Some days are just hard. It's difficult to see through the dark, to see a path forward when everything feels hopeless. But even in the dark, we can find joy—because God is always with us and it's in His presence that we find true joy, no matter the difficulty surrounding us.

God knows the way in the dark because He *is* the Way through the dark—the Light for our paths. And He is with us at all times, His very presence is our comfort and joy through it all.

Even on the days when life feels like a big mess, when it's hard and it hurts and you can't see how on earth any of this can be "good," God has not stopped working. He has not stopped making a way. He has not stopped loving you.

So you can breathe deep today and know that, no matter what you're facing, *all* things are still working together for your ultimate good and His ultimate glory (Romans 8:28).

You will show me the way of life, granting me the joy of your presence and the pleasures of living with you forever.

PSALM 16:11

inhale:

SHOW ME THE
WAY OF LIFE,

exhale:

GIVE ME THE
JOY OF YOUR
PRESENCE.

ALL GOODNESS COMES FROM GOD

Breathe Deep and Know: *All the good in your life is from God. You can trust His sovereign love for you.*

Take a minute to acknowledge your complete dependence on God.

Does it bring you comfort or anxiety when you think about God's sovereignty? Do you feel joy or fear at the thought of being dependent on Him for every good thing in your life? Most of us tend to want some level of control—we want to plan and dictate how our days will go and what the outcomes will be. Deep down (whether we realize it or not), we believe that if we work hard enough or do enough good things, then blessings will come to us. If that doesn't happen, or if the circumstances in our lives are out of our control, anxiety, fear, and worry can fill our minds.

But if we recognize that, all along, God is the one in control, and if we trust that He is good and that He loves us, we can let go of that desperate need to control everything, and we can have peace no matter what comes our way.

All of life becomes an opportunity for joy when we see every bit of it as a gift from our good and loving God.

I say to the Lord, "You are my Lord;
I have no good apart from you."
PSALM 16:2 ESV

inhale:
You are
my Lord;

exhale:
I have
no good
apart
from You.

YOU ARE SECURE IN CHRIST

Breathe Deep and Know: *Your life is safe in Christ. You are no longer bound by the chains of your sin. You are free to live by faith. You are loved and secure in Jesus.*

Here's some really good news to focus on today: Jesus loves you so much that He gave His life for you. He died, was buried, and rose again to give you new life. If you've trusted in Him, though your soul was dead without Christ, you are now alive with His fresh breath of salvation. Your sins are forgiven; you've been set free! And the Holy Spirit has already begun to integrate all that was disintegrated, to remake all that was broken, to restore all that was lost, to loose the chains that bound you to sin, and to make all things gloriously new!

You no longer have to live bound by fear or shame. You can now live guided by faith, trusting that the One who saved you is the One who sustains you and holds you securely in His loving hands. No worry, no fear, no hard thing or dark day can undo what He has done or change His love for you. Not today. Not ever.

I have been crucified with Christ. It is no longer I who live, but Christ who lives in me. And the life I now live in the flesh I live by faith in the Son of God, who loved me and gave himself for me.

GALATIANS 2:20 ESV

inhale:

I LIVE BY FAITH IN YOU,

exhale:

YOU LOVE ME AND GAVE
YOURSELF FOR ME.

GOD IS YOUR HOPE WHEN
YOU'RE DISCOURAGED

Breathe Deep and Know: *Discouragement
is an opportunity to remember God,
to remember all that He has done, and to
remind your soul that He isn't finished yet.*

Sometimes it seems like the world around me is dancing and I can't hear the song. Everyone else appears to be moving right along in a quick choreography of a happy life, and I haven't been given any choreography at all. In the dark seasons of my soul, the slow cadence of suffering is the rhythm of my days. Maybe those of you with chronic pain or mental health conditions can relate. It is so easy to become discouraged when the suffering lingers or the hurt is slow to heal, when prayers for healing aren't answered the way we want them to be.

That's when we remember God. We remember His presence, His goodness, His love. We train our minds to turn to Him. And when the brutal beat of discouragement drums on, we remember that He holds us through every stanza of suffering until a chorus of victory breaks through. God is still writing your story, and nothing is wasted—it is all working together into a beautiful composition that will ultimately sing of His goodness and glory.

---

*My God! Now I am deeply discouraged,
but I will remember you.*

PSALM 42:6

INHALE:

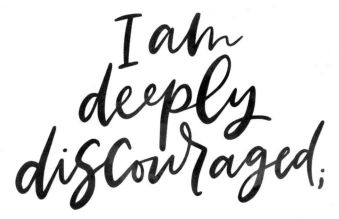

I am
deeply
discouraged;

EXHALE:

but I will
remember
You.

GOD HAS THE ANSWERS

Breathe Deep and Know: *You may not always know what to do, but you can always turn your eyes to the One who does.*

Sometimes the circumstances of our lives seem bigger than we can possibly manage. Like a vast and powerful army, our struggles and difficulties seem impossible to conquer. What do we do when we don't know what to do? When the problems are too big and the fear is too strong?

We turn our eyes to the One who is bigger and stronger than all of it. We turn our eyes to the One who loves us and holds us and is making a way for us, even when it seems impossible. He's the Master of doing the impossible after all. Our impossible situations are really opportunities to turn to Him and trust Him and to watch Him do what only He can do. But first, we must take our eyes off of the army—off that really hard thing in front of us—and put them fully and steadily on God.

What big impossible thing are you facing today? It's ok if you don't know what to do. Simply put your eyes on Christ and let Him lead.

For we have no power to face this vast army that is attacking us. We do not know what to do, but our eyes are on you.
2 CHRONICLES 20:12 NIV

inhale:

I don't know what to do;

exhale:

but my eyes are on You.

GOD'S WAYS ARE HIGHER

Breathe Deep and Know: *God knows what He's doing even if you don't understand it. You can trust Him.*

If we were holding the pen, we'd probably write our stories differently. Perhaps we'd edit out a particular section that wasn't pleasant or skip over a bit that required some learning and growth. But His ways are not our ways, and His thoughts are not our thoughts.

Trying to understand the ways of God is like trying to describe the depths of the entire ocean by studying only a single drop of seawater. There is just so much we can't see, so much we don't know, and so much God has in store for us that we'll comprehend only when we see Him face to face.

So when circumstances don't make sense, when you have more questions than answers, when you don't understand what God is doing, remember that He sees far more than you can and His thoughts are far higher than yours. You may never be able to fully understand the ways of God, but you don't have to. You can trust that His ways are for your good, to bring you closer to Him and to grow you in holiness.

"My thoughts are nothing like your thoughts," says the Lord. "And my ways are far beyond anything you could imagine. For just as the heavens are higher than the earth, so my ways are higher than your ways and my thoughts higher than your thoughts."

ISAIAH 55:8–9

inhale:

YOUR THOUGHTS
ARE NOT
MY THOUGHTS,

exhale:

YOUR WAYS ARE
HIGHER THAN MINE.

GOD CANNOT BE SHAKEN

Breathe Deep and Know: *Your unchanging God is right beside you, keeping you safe and unshaken.*

———————

God doesn't promise specific timelines for our struggles, and He doesn't say that He will spare us from suffering or pain. But He does promise His presence. And He promises that He will give us rest. He will comfort us—not when we make it to the other side of our suffering but right in the messy middle of it all. And He can give you peace even if the struggles that surround you don't change—because *He can change you*, from the inside out. And you can know His peace when life is like shifting sand—because He stays the same.

God's character is constant. He is good, compassionate, gracious, faithful, loving, just, holy, patient, kind, merciful, and wise.

Nothing that happens in this world,

Nothing that happens in your life,

nothing at all, ever, not now or anything to come,

will ever change the character of God.

Your faith can be unmoving even when your world is shaking if your foundation is rooted in the unchanging character of God instead of on the shifting sands of circumstances.

———————

I know the Lord *is always with me. I will not be shaken, for he is right beside me. No wonder my heart is glad, and I rejoice. My body rests in safety.*

PSALM 16:8–9

INHALE:
You are always with me;

EXHALE:
I will not be shaken.

INHALE:
You are right beside me,

EXHALE:
and I am safe.

YOU CAN SLEEP IN PEACE

Breathe Deep and Know: *You can sleep in safety because God is with you.*

Are you ever afraid to go to sleep? Or do you find it difficult to fall asleep because your mind is racing, filled with a million worries? Insomnia is a pretty common symptom of anxiety. It can be difficult to quiet those anxious thoughts when all is still and dark around you. Nighttime can be the loneliest and scariest time of the day for some people.

We are vulnerable when we sleep—unable to defend against the onslaughts of life. But our bodies naturally *require* time to shut down and rest. God intentionally wired us to need sleep, to set down our need for control for a few hours every day and trust that He will keep us safe.

This is a great breath prayer to pray as you lie down to sleep. Breathe deeply and slowly. Pay attention to the rhythm of your breath. Perhaps even place your hand on your stomach so you can feel it expand with each breath. Then pray the words of this prayer, and remind your soul that God is with you and that He can keep you safe.

In peace I will lie down and sleep,
for you alone, O Lord, will keep me safe.

PSALM 4:8

inhale:

I WILL SLEEP IN PEACE,

exhale:

FOR YOU WILL
KEEP ME SAFE.

GOD IS MAKING A WAY

Breathe Deep and Know: *You don't have to fear what today may bring because you know the One who is making a way and can trust Him to lead you through.*

Are you in the middle of a circumstance or a season that hasn't gone at all the way you expected? Does the path you're on right now look nothing like you thought it would?

Expectations can lead to disappointment when things don't work out the way we think they should. Uncertainty about the future can lead to much anxiety when our hearts are full of worry.

Trusting God means trusting Him to lead and make a way forward—even when the path ahead is unclear. A certain kind of contentment comes from trusting the heart of God, from learning to hold what you have loosely and accept with gratitude whatever comes.

God loves you. Whatever happens, He is with you. Whatever He gives, it is a gift. It is all grace upon grace, gift upon gift from your Maker who loves you and will do whatever it takes to draw you closer to His heart, to His way, to His side.

Lead me, Lord, in your righteousness because of my enemies—make your way straight before me.

PSALM 5:8 NIV

inhale:

LEAD ME IN YOUR
RIGHTEOUSNESS;

exhale:

MAKE YOUR WAY
STRAIGHT BEFORE ME.

GOD RENEWS YOUR STRENGTH

Breathe Deep and Know: *Your strength will be renewed as you put your trust in God.*

How's your strength today? Are you feeling strong in your spirit? Or are you feeling weak and weary? Do you feel worn down by your circumstances, your health, your life? Has a battle you've been fighting depleted your strength?

That weariness you feel is a signal, a sign that something is not aligned—in your body, your soul, or both. Make time to slow down today and allow God to renew your strength as you realign your heart with His. Even if the physical symptoms of your weariness do not go away, especially if you are living with a chronic illness or health condition, your spirit can still be strong and your soul can be renewed. The first step to this renewal is to turn toward God and to trust Him. Trust God with your circumstances, your health, your life. Trust Him with that battle you're facing. Give Him your weariness, turn to His Word, and let the truth of His promises renew your heart and mind as you trust Him today.

But those who trust in the Lord will find new strength.
They will soar high on wings like eagles.
They will run and not grow weary.
They will walk and not faint.

ISAIAH 40:31

inhale:

I trust you, Lord;

exhale:

Renew my strength.

THERE IS HOPE IN THE WAITING

Breathe Deep and Know: *There is always hope when you are waiting, because God can be trusted to always keep His word.*

Seasons of waiting can be painfully long and hard. But waiting time is not wasted time. God wastes nothing. He is always doing something. God is working as we wait, regardless of whether we can see or understand what He is doing.

Not only is He working through the circumstances around us, but He is working *within* us, preparing and shaping us as we wait. Because of this, we can always have hope. Tish Harrison Warren says, "To hope is to 'borrow grace.' It is not naive optimism. Hope admits the truth of our vulnerability. It does not trust God to keep all bad things from happening. But it assumes that redemption, beauty, and goodness will be there for us, whatever lies ahead."[19] God's Word is our hope in the waiting, because His Word reminds us that He is with us and that He always keeps His word.

What are you waiting for today? Root your hope in God's Word as you wait, and let His promises give you peace.

I wait for the LORD, my soul waits,
and in his word I hope.

PSALM 130:5 ESV

inhale:
I wait for you,
Lord;

exhale:
My hope is in
your Word.

GOD'S LOVE IS UNFAILING

Breathe Deep and Know: *God's unfailing, faithful love is with you every day. You can trust Him to show you the way.*

The love and kindness of God is unshakable and ever faithful. God doesn't love you because you follow Him; He loves you because He loves you. Period. He isn't kind because you trust Him; He is kind because He is kind. Period. It's who He is.

God's love isn't dependent upon the circumstances in your life. His kindness is not limited by your struggles or suffering. He is with you *in* your suffering—not in spite of it or because He has to be. God is right there within your suffering, coming alongside you as your Friend. Faith grows not despite the hard things; it grows *because of* the hard things. It's often in the darkest moments when God's presence is the sweetest. It's often in the hardest times that His love is most tender.

God loves you *today*. You can trust Him with your whole life—the good and the hard and everything in between. Begin today remembering His faithful love and placing your life in His hands.

Let the morning bring me word of your unfailing love, for I have put my trust in you. Show me the way I should go, for to you I entrust my life.

PSALM 143:8 NIV

inhale:

LET THE MORNING
BRING ME WORD

exhale:

OF YOUR UNFAILING,
FAITHFUL LOVE.

inhale:

SHOW ME THE WAY I
SHOULD GO,

exhale:

I TRUST YOU WITH MY
WHOLE LIFE.

GOD MEETS YOUR EVERY NEED

Breathe Deep and Know: *God gives you breath and life.*
You can trust that He will meet your every need.

The breath of God is the source of all life. In the beginning, God breathed the breath of life into man and the soul came alive.

Even now, it's His breath that moves in and out of our lungs, flows through every vessel and vein in our bodies, and gives life to every one of our organs and cells.

It's the breath of God that gives you life, and it's His breath that sustains it.

If God can make life from His breath, can't He do anything? If He can birth stars and galaxies with a word, and give life and breath to everything on this beautiful planet, can't He meet any need you may have today?

Breathe in right now and be reminded of the gift of life God has given you. Inhale His love and goodness deep into our soul.

Now exhale all your worries and fears. Breathe out whatever is weighing you down and let the breath of God fill you with renewed peace as you trust Him to meet all of your needs.

He himself gives life and breath to everything,
and he satisfies every need.

ACTS 17:25

inhale:

You give life and breath
to everything,

exhale:

You satisfy my every need.

NOTES

1. Curt Thompson MD, *Anatomy of the Soul: Surprising Connections between Neuroscience and Spiritual Practices That Can Transform Your Life and Relationships* (Carol Stream, IL: Tyndale, 2010), xvii.

2. For information on the differences between worry and anxiety, see "Worry and Anxiety: Do You Know the Difference?" *Henry Ford Health*, August 2020, www.henryford.com/blog/2020/08/the-difference-between-worry-and-anxiety.

3. Phillip Low MD, "Overview of the Autonomic Nervous System," *College of Medicine*, Mayo Clinic, Sept 2021, www.merckmanuals.com/home/brain ,-spinal-cord,-and-nerve-disorders/autonomic-nervous-system-disorders /overview-of-the-autonomic-nervous-system.

4. Thompson, *Anatomy of the Soul*, 42.

5. Further information on this entire process can be found at "Understanding the Stress Response," Harvard Health Publishing, Harvard Medical School, July 2020, www.health.harvard.edu/staying-healthy/understanding-the-stress-response.

6. The terms "emotional brain" and "thinking brain" are from "What Happens in the Brain When We Feel Fear," *Smithsonian Magazine*, October 2017, www.smithsonianmag.com/science-nature/what-happens-brain-feel-fear-180966992/.

7. Information taken from Will Meek PhD, "The Difference Between Normal Anxiety and GAD," *Very Well Mind*, December 2020, www.verywellmind.com/the -difference-between-normal-anxiety-and-gad-1393143 and "Anxiety Disorders," National Institute of Mental Health, www.nimh.nih.gov/health/topics/anxiety -disorders.

8. Thompson, *Anatomy of the Soul*, 42.

9. This information about the vagus nerve is from "Understanding the Stress Response," *Harvard Health*, www.health.harvard.edu/staying-healthy /understanding-the-stress-response and "Everything you need to know about the

vagus nerve," *Medical News Today*, www.medicalnewstoday.com/articles/318128 #What-is-the-vagus-nerve.

10. The term "dis-integrated" is from Thompson, *Anatomy of the Heart*, 184.

11. The phrase "breathing is the bridge between mind and body" is from "Breathing: An Introduction," *Dr. Weil*, www.drweil.com/health-wellness/body-mind-spirit /stress-anxiety/breathing-an-introduction/.

12. Thompson, *Anatomy of the Heart*, 29.

13. "Best Breathing Techniques for Relaxation and Pain Relief," *Psychology Today*, www.psychologytoday.com/us/blog/finding-new-home/202103/best-breathing -techniques-relaxation-and-pain-relief.

14. Christophe Andre, "Proper Breathing Brings Better Health," *Scientific American*, January 2019, www.scientificamerican.com/article/proper-breathing-brings -better-health/.

15. Xiao Ma, et al., "The Effect of Diaphragmatic Breathing on Attention, Negative Affect and Stress in Healthy Adults," *National Libraries of Medicine*, June 2017, www.ncbi.nlm.nih.gov/pmc/articles/PMC5455070/.

16. Ann Voskamp, *One Thousand Gifts* (Grand Rapids, MI: Zondervan), 65–66.

17. The concept of "amygdala hijacking" from Olivia Guy-Evans, "Amygdala Hijack and the Fight or Flight Response," *Simply Psychology*, www.simplypsychology.org /what-happens-during-an-amygdala-hijack.html.

18. Timothy Keller, *Prayer* (New York: Penguin, 2016), 101.

19. Tish Harrison Warren, *Prayer in the Night* (Downers Grove, IL: InterVarsity Press, 2021), 152.